D0331926

THE CYCLIST'S GUIDE TO NEW YORK CITY

**Marci Blackman,
Ed Glazar,**
and
Michael Green

Skyhorse Publishing

Skyhorse Publishing books may be purchased in bulk at special discounts for sales promotion, corporate gifts, fund-raising, or educational purposes. Special editions can also be created to specifications. For details, contact the Special Sales Department, Skyhorse Publishing, 307 West 36th Street, 11th Floor, New York, NY 10018 or info@skyhorsepublishing.com.

Skyhorse® and Skyhorse Publishing® are registered trademarks of Skyhorse Publishing, Inc.®, a Delaware corporation.

www.skyhorsepublishing.com

10 9 8 7 6 5 4 3 2 1

Library of Congress Cataloging-in-Publication Data is available on file.
ISBN: 978-1-61608-313-7

Printed in China

CONTENTS

INTRODUCTION

A year and a half ago, when Ed and Michael and I sat down to discuss making this book, we asked each other's reasons for wanting to do so. Combined, we have logged close to two hundred thousand miles on these streets, so the answer was easy: "Because the only way to see this city is by bicycle!" Not just *see* the greatest city in the world, but as more and more riders are discovering every day, to really experience it, to breathe it, to feel its heartbeat, you have to ride it. We had plenty of other reasons too, but that was number one.

With all the new cyclists taking to the streets (over two hundred thousand to date), we thought it would be a good idea to share some of the collective knowledge that has kept us hammering all these years. To draw the curtain back, so to speak. Bike messenger lore aside, it's a lot easier and safer to ride here than people think, especially with the increasing number of designated bike lanes (over two hundred miles in the last two years). You just have to be smart about it.

As tour guides we wondered, "How well do those who ride really know this city?" Not just the quickest routes uptown, or from Bed-Stuy to Elmhurst. On a bike it is possible to travel through ten neighborhoods on the way to your destination, more depending on where you're going. Ten distinctly different communities, some the size of small cities, countries in other parts of the world. Not underground. Not in a car, or on a bus, insulated from it all. But out in the open, through it.

To be sure, most New Yorkers know at least a little something: Statue of Liberty, Empire State Building, favorite bar, the neighborhood in which they live, where they work. But what about the others? The hoods you roll through on your way? How each came into being? What went down there? Wouldn't it be cool to spin past 778 Driggs Avenue in Williamsburg and know that the real Frank Serpico was shot there? Or that the New York Life Insurance building, the one with the gilded roof on Madison and Park avenues, was the site of the first two Madison Square Gardens. As a city like no other, New York has a history all its own, and knowing it as you ride enriches the exploration tenfold.

To that end, we have mapped out some of our favorite rides through all five boroughs. Along the way, we ply you with histories, fun-filled facts and urban myths and legends about the sites and neighborhoods through which you are riding, equip you with useful on-route information including bike shop and bathroom locations, popular local eateries and quick-fix electrolyte stops. And in our "On the Wheel" photo profiles, we put faces to a few of the city's two hundred thousand-plus daily cyclists, some of whom have been at it even longer than we have. Part guide book, photo gallery, history, and human interest story, it is our hope that you will enjoy *Bike NYC: The Cyclist's Guide to New York City* as much as we enjoyed creating it.

For updates, route changes, laws, and a complete listing of bike shops by borough, please check out the Bike NYC website at www.bikenycthe-book.com

Ride Safe!

SAFETY TIPS:

1. Here are a few tips about the grid: in general, odd-numbered one-way streets run from east to west, or toward the Hudson, even numbers to the east. Fifth Avenue is the demarcation line between east and west, and to let you in a little bike messenger secret, addresses radiate outward from 5th Avenue in either direction in blocks of one hundred. In other words, 0–99 West 31st Street falls between 5th Avenue and Broadway, 100–199 between Broadway and 6th, and so forth.

2. Avoiding the Door. Dooring is the most frequent type of collision between vehicles and cyclists in NYC. Here are some tips to avoid the door.

- The city is full of livery including yellow cabs, limousines, black cars for corporate clients, and a slew of other car services. Most often drivers do not exit the vehicle but more frequently, passengers will exit from the back door on the curb side. Therefore, it is best to avoid going in between the parked car and the curb, even if it means going into the heavier flow of traffic on the other side.
- Swing wide; ride approximately four feet from car doors on both sides. Bike lanes are roughly four feet in width, so if they are present, use the painted white strip on the outer part of the lane as a way of gauging distance.
- Avoid parked cabs. Yellow cabs looking for a new fare will switch their lights on top to white, signaling that they are available. Parked cabs with their lights off indicate that there are passengers still inside and could pop out at any second. If possible try and gauge how many passengers are in the car and whether the street side of the cab is also a danger.
- You can use side mirrors of vehicles to determine if there are occupants in the vehicle. You can also look for signs such as brake lights on or, in the winter, car exhaust identifying that the vehicle has an occupant.
- Assume nothing. Cyclists can get doored in the middle of the street from cab drivers with no passengers dumping out their cold coffee or when passengers decide there is too much traffic and want to get out. Be aware, and try as much as possible to give yourself distance from all motor vehicles.

3. "Salmoning." Popular satirical blogger the Bike Snob (www. bikesnobnyc.blogspot.com) coined the phrase "salmoning" for people going the wrong way down a one-way street. Don't be a fish.

4. Intersections. Intersections are the most common place where accidents occur. Be super aware of your actions and motorists when navigating them. Do not assume motorists will signal when making turns or are aware of your presence. For example, if you are in the left-turn lane of a busy intersection, ride to the right of the vehicles and the lane, which may mean exiting a left-side bike lane. Be on extra alert when navigating near entrances to expressways or motor vehicle entrances to bridges. This is generally when drivers are at their most impatient.

5. Helmets. ALWAYS WEAR A HELMET!

It's the law for children:

VTL § 1238 (a) Children under fourteen but older than five must wear an approved helmet.

Additional resources: The Bicycle Helmet Safety Institute—www. bhsi.org.

6. Ride with Predictability. Ride with predictability, in a straight line. Use hand signals to alert drivers when changing lanes or trying to work your way across a street. Pointing in the direction you want to go works fine.

7. Debunking Misconceptions. We thought we would debunk a few misconceptions of the laws pertaining to cyclists in NYC.

- It is against the law for an adult to not wear a helmet. False. Only children fourteen years and younger are required to wear a helmet.
- You must ride in bike lanes. The law (—34 RCNY[NYC] 4–12[p][1] states that bicyclists should ride in **usable** bike lanes, unless they are

preparing to turn, or are avoiding unsafe conditions (including but not limited to fixed or moving objects, motor vehicles, bicycles, pedestrians, pushcarts, animals, surface hazards). This law should be applied at the discretion of the cyclist.

- It's illegal to lock your bike to a city street sign. False. You can lock your bike to any city property.
- It is illegal to operate a bicycle drunk. False … sort of. Just because current drunk driving laws apply only to motor vehicles doesn't make cycling inebriated a good idea, especially in New York City.

8. Warning Device. The law (New York State): VTL 1236 (b) Bicycles must have a bell or other audible signal.

Although it is required by law to have a working bell or other warning device on your bike, this law is unlikely to be enforced unless you are stopped by the NYPD for something else and have upset them in some way. However, having a bell is a good idea to signal to pedestrians that you are coming. As stated in our "Bombin' Broadway" chapter, warning devices can often be muted out by general street noise. A whistle or a good yell can sometimes be much more effective.

9. Headphones. The law (NYS): VLT 375 24 (a) Use of earphones while driving or riding a bicycle. It shall be unlawful to operate upon any public highway in this state a bicycle while the operator is wearing more than one earphone.

Why it's a good idea (not to wear them): Riding to your favorite music may seem like a good idea, but NYC requires the use of all senses. Being able to hear traffic and emergency vehicles is part of being alert on the bicycle.

10. Avoid Sidewalks. The law (Administrative Code-NYC): AC 19-176–Riding bicycles on sidewalks is prohibited. Bicycles may be confiscated.

Why it's a good idea (not to): sidewalk riding is the number one complaint of pedestrians, as well as a favored summons by police.

11. Ride with Confidence. Own the lane. Ride confidently. It is always good to look around and know what is behind you, but constant looking back and hesitation can send the wrong message to motorists. Get comfortable in your space.

12. Pedestrians. Jaywalking is not enforced in NYC. Pedestrians dart out from every direction and they are often distracted by other things such as texting or talking on cell phones. Give pedestrians space. When pedestrians are crossing roadways, always pass behind them.

13. Lights. The law: Vehicle and traffic law for New York State—VTL 1236 (a) and (e) Bicycles must have a white headlight, a red taillight, and reflectors between dusk and dawn.

Why it's a good idea: Although NYC is a fairly bright city, cyclists feel more confident when they are seen, especially at night and in bad weather. It also helps to be more visible to other cyclists and sometimes bridge paths have sections with broken lights. Remember, white light goes in the front, red in the back.

CHAPTER 1

THE CLOISTERS—MANHATTAN
TIP TO TIP (Twenty-six Miles)

The Museum

The Cloisters is the branch of the Metropolitan Museum of Art that houses its collection of medieval art and culture. Located on a rocky bluff overlooking the Hudson River near the upper tip of Manhattan in Fort Tryon Park, an auxiliary site in the Battle of Fort Washington during the American Revolutionary War, the museum is named for the columned arcades known as *cloisters* that form the basis of its medieval structure and design. The arcades—acquired (some might argue stolen) in the early twentieth century by sculptor-turned-art-dealer and collector George Grey Barnard—are sections of the larger cloisters taken from four medieval monasteries in France. In need of money, in 1925 Barnard sold his collection, including the cloisters, to the Metropolitan Museum of Art, who received the funds to obtain it from John D. Rockefeller Jr. Several years earlier, Rockefeller had already purchased the sixty-seven-acre former Revolutionary War site from Union Carbide founder, C. K. G. Billings (remember the Bhopal disaster?), and hired Frederick Law Olmsted Jr., son of the designer of Central, Morningside, and Prospect parks, to landscape it. Five years after acquiring the Barnard collection, Rockefeller donated the designated parkland to the city, reserving the bluff overlooking the Hudson for a museum to house the Met's new collection of late medieval art.

Among some five thousand works on display here, the cornerstones of the collection are the *Unicorn Tapestries*—seven woven 15th-century wall hangings, donated by Rockefeller himself, depicting the *Hunt of the Unicorn*. In addition to the gardens within the museum's walls, there are

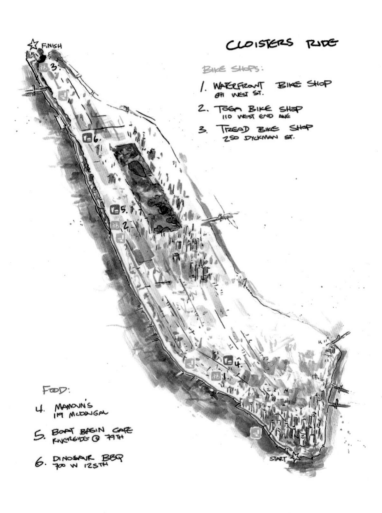

CLOISTERS RIDE

BIKE SHOPS:

1. WATERFRONT BIKE SHOP
   391 WEST ST.

2. TOGA BIKE SHOP
   110 WEST END AVE

3. TREAD BIKE SHOP
   250 DYCKMAN ST.

FOOD:

4. MAMOUN'S
   119 McDOUGAL

5. BOAT BASIN CAFE
   RIVERSIDE @ 79TH

6. DINOSAUR BBQ
   700 W 125TH

FINISH

START

also footpaths you can walk to explore the grounds without that wind down around the bluff through the wooded and rocky meadows of Fort Tryon, where visitors can gaze at the breathtaking New Jersey shoreline and Palisades, the forested cliffs on the other side of the river—also purchased by Rockefeller to guarantee unspoiled views of tranquility. If you are lucky, you might even catch a glimpse of Matt Damon lurking around (as Bike NYC did while photographing this ride), or some other celebrity, shooting scenes for their latest film. The eerie 15th-century setting is a favorite for moviemakers.

After taking in the museum and touring the grounds and gardens, enjoy a well-earned meal or drink at the park's New Leaf Restaurant and Bar, restored and managed by the New York Restoration Project—a. k. a Bette Midler and friends. The restaurant is a bit on the pricey side though. If money is an object, you will fare better at one of the local Latin joints or food stands, like *Patacon Pisao* on 202nd Street, or *El Floridita* at 4162 Broadway, in neighboring Inwood or Washington Heights. While the museum and collection are enjoyable year-round, the surrounding park and palisades are most spectacular in the fall, during the peak of the foliage change.

The Ride

First things first. Are your tires pumped up? Brakes grabbing properly? Seat height correct? Do you have enough water, or Gatorade, or other electrolyte replenisher? Camera? Money? What snacks and tools, or gear, did you pack in your bag?

Start at the southern tip of Manhattan, the plaza between Robert F. Wagner Jr. Park and Pier A, a jutting peninsula where the East and Hudson rivers converge with the salt-laced swells of the Atlantic to form the historic panoramic New York Harbor. If you are facing south

toward the water, on your left is the 122-year-old Pier A, the old fireboat station (currently undergoing restoration), and the twenty-five-acre-plus Battery Park, site of the original Southwest Battery and Castle Clinton.

Named for former mayor and governor DeWitt Clinton, Castle Clinton is one of four American forts still standing constructed to defend the island during the buildup to the War of 1812. The others are Fort Jay and Castle Williams on Governors Island (to the east) and Fort Wood, the star-pointed foundation of the Statue of Liberty on Liberty Island (formerly Bedloe's Island) about a half mile south in front of you. After the war, Castle Clinton was renamed Castle Garden and operated by the city as an entertainment complex, housing in succession a promenade and beer garden, New York's first theater district, which eventually gave rise to Time's Square and Broadway, and from 1855 to 1890, the state's first Emigration Depot, where more than eight million immigrants filtered through its gates before Ellis Island replaced it in 1892. Further south, beyond Liberty and Governors islands lies Staten Island, the last county incorporated into New York's five boroughs. The old Jersey Rail Yard, the recently developed Jersey City skyline, and the 1,964-square-foot Colgate Clock, erected in 1924 on the former site of the Colgate-Palmolive toothpaste and soap factory, line the banks on the western shore of the river.

To begin, follow along the Hudson, heading north, making sure to ride on the pathway nearest the water (the upper path is for walking only). Before it was the Hudson, the body of water you see had a different name—*Muheakantack* was the *Lenape* native word for "the river that flows both ways." You'll get a great view of the river as it weaves around the quays and bridge of the South Cove playground beneath the Oz-like towers and skyscrapers of the financial district shimmering overhead to the tree and garden-lined Esplanade below. If you are renting, use this first quarter mile of the ride to become familiar with your bike. Visiting? Holler at a few pedestrians to get the F—— out of your way so you can feel like a true New Yorker. Be careful which bipeds you choose to accost, though, and prepare for something equally obnoxious, if not worse, to be hollered in turn. Welcome to New York!

Continue along the Esplanade past sculptor Ned Smyth's "Upper Room," an elevated 34 x 67–foot colonnaded open temple, lording over the river like a restored and modernized ancient ruin. After the "Upper Room," **spin past the volleyball court around the North Cove Harbor**, home to the Manhattan Yacht-Club and Sailing School, and the three-and-half-acre plaza to the World Financial Center. (Will Smith fans might recognize the cove from the 2005 romantic comedy *Hitch* in which Smith plays a "date doctor" for an unlucky cadre of bachelors unable to hook up). **If there is an issue with your bike (seat height adjustment, flat tire),** this is a good place to address it. In addition to the nautical majesty of yachts and sailboats pitching on the swells, the river and the Jersey City skyline beyond, there are cafés, restaurants, public restrooms, as well as the best view going these days of the sobering site of Ground Zero from the top of the atrium inside the Financial Center.

No need or desire to stop? **Wrap around the harbor to the left, back toward the water past the Mercantile Exchange, and drop down the ramp to the right,** again keeping to the lower shared pathway. Follow along the waterfront past the Port Authority Ferry Terminal and the Irish Hunger Memorial opposite artist Brian Tolle's 2002 homage to the victims and survivors of Ireland's nineteenth century Potato Famine.

An authentic famine-era abandoned cottage, imported and recon-structed stone by stone, the soil outside the memorial has been planted with native Irish flora—in particular, the vegetation that grows in unsown fields. On the inside, the base of the memorial is wrapped in layers of frosted glass and fossilized limestone, with ghostlike bands of text hover-ing beneath the surface. As you read the inscription, voices whispering in surround sound chronicle the bleak and arid famine as well as modern-day hunger crises still wreaking havoc throughout the world.

Just past the Hunger Memorial at the entrance to Nelson A. Rock-efeller Park lives the city's new and improved Poets House, a dedicated place for readers and writers of "world-class poetry."

Founded in 1985 by two-time United States Poet Laureate, Stanley Kunitz, and New York patron saint of poets, Elizabeth Kray, this sanctuary for all things verse nurtures a library boasting a collection of over fifty thousand titles. In addition to housing hard-hitting, cutting-edge chapbooks, CDs and DVDs alongside volumes sung to us by Pulitzer and Nobel prize winners, Poets House offers an elegant meeting room as well as a fjord of inspiration inside and out. In the tradition of New York's long-impassioned commitment to the arts, Poet's House is one of Battery Park City's "rent-free" residents, with a lease that will not come up for renewal until 2069.

At the end of Rockefeller Park (the North Meadow), follow the path to the right past Stuyvesant High School, one of three advanced public secondary schools overseen by the NYC Board of Education to "serve the needs of the academically gifted." The other two are the Bronx High School of Science and the Brooklyn Technical High School. Together they are known as the specialized science high schools, where the emphasis of study is on math, science, and technology. While tuition to these schools is free, in order to gain entrance, students must earn superior scores on a special admittance exam. Counted among Stuyvesant's hundreds of notable alumni are legendary jazz pianist, composer, and pioneer Thelonious Monk; President Barack Obama's senior advisor and campaign guru David Axelrod; present attorney general of the United States, Eric H. Holder; and actress Lucy Liu.

After passing Stuyvesant, turn left (north) onto the Hudson River Greenway, a two-way, two-lane, bike path completely separated from traffic, which runs from the southern tip of Manhattan to the north. Completed in 2003, this thirteen-mile continuous pathway—along with its near-finished cousins along the East and Harlem rivers—represents the borough of Manhattan's contribution to the longer truly ambitious East Coast Greenway—a 2,500-mile protected bike lane, connecting urban centers on the eastern seaboard from Florida to Maine.

As you ride, make sure to look around you. Inhale the pulse of the city: the exhaust of the taxi cabs and cars, the garbage trucks erratically honking and whizzing by at the frenetic pace of mosquitoes on crack on the adjacent West Side Highway, ambulance sirens blaring—always—in the too-near distance. Taste the dreams and drive and resilience hanging on the air like condensation, the conveyor belt of belief on which this chaotic metropolis moves and thrives—a quiet collective unwavering faith that anything is possible here. If you work for it. Feel it on your skin, the grit and grime of three hundred and eighty-five years of desire and determination. Behold the island of *Mannahatta*, the Empire State Building orchestrating the skyline as neighborhood after neighborhood unfolds before you like movements in a concerto.

As you coast north, the first neighborhood you encounter is **TriBeCa**—the **Tri**angle **be**low **Ca**nal Street. Home of the TriBeCa International Film Festival, and a one-time bohemian mecca, Tribeca's artists' lofts and warehouses are now mostly occupied by celebrities. (Formerly known as Washington Market, the neighborhood holds the distinction as the city's first residential community before the Industrial Revolution commercialized it during the nineteenth century.)

Since reentry by the rich and famous, at one time or another TriBeCa has been called home by Leonardo DiCaprio, Uma Thurman, John F. Kennedy Jr., Mike D of Beastie Boy fame, Gwyneth Paltrow, Jay-Z, Beyoncé, and many others, including Robert De Niro, co-owner of the neighborhood's trendy TriBeCa Grill on Greenwich Street.

Yet the brightest star in the neighborhood—it could be argued—is the Holland Tunnel. Along with the Lincoln Tunnel further uptown, the Holland Tunnel is one of two underwater highways connecting Manhattan to the state of New Jersey. Completed in 1927, the little-over-a-mile-and-a-half (2.6 km) engineering marvel is one of the earliest tunnels in the world constructed with a ventilation system. The first of its kind in the United States, the system uses eighty-four fans housed in four separate ventilation buildings that stretch out across the Hudson like concrete sentries on a rise. From Canal Street in Manhattan to 12th Street in Jersey City, these fans simultaneously draw fresh air in and push car exhaust out. Regularly tested throughout its existence, the air inside the Holland Tunnel has often been found to be cleaner than that of the cities it connects. In addition, the tunnel has developed something of a presence in Hollywood screenwriting. It has been featured in several movies, including *Daylight* and *Ghostbusters* I and II (for all you Harold Ramis fanatics out there, the Hook & Ladder #8 Firehouse on Varick Street and North Moore provided the legendary façade of the *Ghostbusters* movie headquarters).

In 2007, the Holland Tunnel was forever engraved into the cornerstone of local bike culture lore when fledgling bicycle messenger Brendan McMullen was nearly taken to jail after racing end to end on his Huffy 10-speed to deliver a rush package to New Jersey. McMullen had been told by dispatch that the pickup was going to an address on Hudson Street in the city, but when he arrived to pick it up, he discovered it was actually going to Hudson Street in Jersey City, and had to be there in less than thirty minutes. What's the fastest route from downtown Manhattan to Jersey City by bike? The Holland Tunnel. Reportedly, weaving in and out of traffic faster than the cars, McMullen made it across in under five minutes. (Perhaps the courier was on to something: by car, especially during rush hour, the journey can take upwards of an hour.) For all McMullen's quick thinking and effort, however, when he emerged on the Jersey side of the tunnel, he was met by Port Authority Police officers and arrested. Fortunately for Mr. McMullen, after verifying his story with the messenger company as well as the client who sent the package, the police let him off with a ticket and mandatory court appearance. (Tourist note: As of this writing, bicycles are not allowed in the Holland Tunnel. Earnest as it was, Bike NYC would never advocate anyone attempting to duplicate Brendan McMullen's Journey. Ever. Even if it would shave fifty-five minutes off your commute.) As for the package? Dispatch sent out another courier, this time traveling by car, to retrieve and carry it the rest of the way.

As you leave TiBeCa, **ride along the Greenway past the Tunnel's ventilation buildings and the Manhattan Flying Trapeze School on the roof of the Pier 40 parking lot on the left and stop in front of the white bicycle (just past Clarkson Street), with the halo of plywood painted sunflowers arranged around it, chained and padlocked to the street post. It's called a ghost bike**—one of approximately sixty bicycle memorials chained to street signs at intersections throughout the city in memory of fallen cyclists killed by cars.

Inspired by similar programs begun in Pittsburgh and St. Louis a few years earlier, The NYC Street Memorial Project was started in 2005, by the artist-activist collective Visual Resistance. In addition to honoring slain cyclists, the project aims to improve the conditions under which we ride by drawing attention to the preventable and senseless tragedies that too often claim our lives. Each memorial consists of a patchwork, pieced together donated bicycle, spray-painted white, with a small rectangular plaque affixed to the top tube disclosing the rider's name, age, the date of the tragedy, and a brief, painfully inadequate footnote describing what happened. After a somber two-wheeled procession from a designated starting point to the site of the accident, the riderless bicycle borne along like a pall by the handlebars, helmet-clad and messenger-bag-wearing mourners raise bikes overhead (a "bike raising") to remember the fallen as the newly christened ghost bike is chained and padlocked to the street post. One by one, after friends and family share stories and memories of their loved one, fellow cyclists file past the bike to say goodbye. Some tuck flowers and mementos in between spokes and brake cables, under the wheels and tires as they pass. Others light safe-passage candles and place them around the bike as they would an altar. Though a few might cross themselves, or silently whisper a private blessing or prayer, most simply cry, whether a friend of the victim or not, looking on bewildered and sobered at what might just as easily have been a memorial for ourselves.

As riders prepare to pedal back into the day-to-day never-ending hustle of life here, a protest hymn is sometimes played on a lone bugle or trumpet, or lifted up to the sky in a chorus of discordant a capella voices, lost in the ever-deafening din of taxicabs honking, bus engines roaring, sirens wailing, jackhammers pounding, people scurrying about the grid as ants throughout a colony. We point these phantom bicycles out to you, not from a sense of the macabre, nor are we trying to frighten or discourage you in any way from riding. We bring these memorials to your attention to continue to foster visual awareness, remind you to always be alert and careful, and give you an opportunity to pause for a moment in your two-wheeled discovery of this magnificent city to remember the individual riders and organizations who (some with their lives) have made such exploration possible.

This particular ghost bike is dedicated to Eric Ng, a twenty-two-year-old NYU graduate and Brooklyn public school teacher. Friday night, December 1, 2006, Eric was bicycling on the Greenway when he was killed by a drunk driver who, after leaving a holiday party at Chelsea Piers, mistook the narrow two-lane bike path Eric was on for the eight lane Westside Highway adjacent to it.

After the ghost bike, pedal past the Water Front Bicycle Shop and Christopher Street in Greenwich Village, site of the 1969 Stonewall Uprising. Considered by many the birth of America's gay civil rights movement, the uprising began sometime after midnight on June 28, 1969, when New York City police officers rushed into the Stonewall Inn. The Christopher Street gay bar had been run by the mafia for years. At a time when homosexuality and all acts associated with it were illegal, police raids on gay bars were commonplace. But on June 28, 1969, emboldened, perhaps, by the countrywide protest environment against the Vietnam War, the patrons of the Stonewall Inn decided to fight back. Over the next three days, a series of violent riots ensued, prompting the formation of the Gay Liberation Front, the first in what would quickly become a mosh pit of gay and lesbian activist organizations fighting for equal rights.

First settled as a hamlet oasis of sprawling estates by wealthy landowners with colonial era names like De Lancey and Van Cortlandt, like the rest of Manhattan, the city's largest historical district has survived a plethora of geographic and demographic transformations. After a yellow fever epidemic followed by outbreaks of cholera, dysentery, and other communicable diseases forced lower Manhattanites to move north into neighborhoods like the Village, where the air was cleaner, the sprawling estates of the rich were broken up into lots and sold to speculators and developers seeking to profit from the migration. By the time the Stonewall riots ignited the resolve of the city's and nation's gay population, the

Village had gone from a combustible pairing of poor Irish immigrants and working-class African Americans to Italians, and finally to artists and writers and other avant-garde types (including Beat Generation poet William Burroughs).

These days, while the façades remain, many of the old tenements have been gutted and converted into five- and six-story town houses or mansions. The bars, restaurants, and vintage book and clothing shops established in the '50s and '60s replaced by trendy Polo, Coach, and Marc Jacobs stores. A few die-hard holdouts still live on, however, like Mamoun's on McDougal Street, between Bleecker and West 3rd. Since 1971, Mamoun's has been home of the best falafel sandwich in Manhattan. Another not-to-miss classic shop is the old-school Corner Bistro on the corner of West 4th and Jane streets, which has been serving the neighborhood libations and burgers for nearly a century now. The Village Vanguard (7th Avenue between West 11th and Perry streets) is a legend in itself. The world-renowned jazz club opened by Max Gordon in 1935 is now run by his widow, Lorraine. Once called "the most famous basement in the world," the Vanguard has spawned over one hundred live groundbreaking albums recorded by such masters of the craft as Sonny Rollins, John Coltrane, McCoy Tyner, Bill Evans, Dexter Gordon, Art Blakey, Miles Davis, and Wynton Marsalis, to name but a few.

Since 1827 and 1832, respectively, the Village has also been home to Washington Square Park and New York University. Prior to becoming a park, for thirty-one years, the square was a hanging ground and potter's field. As a common gravesite where the city buried its indigent (particularly those swept under by the tide of yellow fever) and capital criminals convicted and sentenced to death by the state, it is estimated that the ground beneath the park still entombs the remains of over twenty thousand dead people, with some placing the number as high as one hundred thousand. In fact, in the location of the 118-year-old Washington Square Arch, a gallows once stood. City residents around the square were treated, routinely, to barbaric public executions. Commuting has always been an issue in New York—not surprisingly it is believed that the hangman lived just steps away, always on call, on the corner of what is now Washington Square North and 5th Avenue.

Continue along the waterfront past the Village and the bike shop, and skirt around the last remaining vestiges of the old Meatpacking District, Manhattan's newest trendy neighborhood, and, historically speaking, one of the more colorful and diverse she has to offer. Encompassing the area between West 14th Street and Gansevoort Street to the south, from Hudson Street west to the Hudson River, the Belgian Block (cobblestone) paved district was originally called Gansevoort Market. Named after the nineteenth-century fort honoring Peter Gansevoort (an officer in the American Revolutionary War and the grandfather of novelist-essayist-poet Herman Melville), the market can trace its humble beginnings back to a *Lenape* Indian trading post. After Henry Hudson took his famous ride up the river, the district morphed from a Dutch tobacco plantation to British farmland, to a farmers' market, and for most of the twentieth century, until the late 1990s, a meatpacking district. For nearly one hundred years over 250 slaughterhouses butchered, trimmed, packaged, and sold meat. Today, only a handful of those vendors remain, and, until recently, animal meat wasn't the only flesh peddled here.

From the late 1960s into the early 1990s, the Belgian Block, low-awning, warehouse-lined streets, attracted some of the city's more scandalous denizens. For those who preferred the area's perceived isolation, ensconced along the waterfront under the abandoned elevated railroad terminus (the new High Line park and promenade), the Belgian Block offered a refuge from the harsh scrutiny of judgmental mainstream eyes. At night after the butchers and taxi mechanics closed up shop and went home to their families, the carcass and oil-imbibed deserted cobblestone streets—where horse hooves once echoed—came alive with the neighs and whinnies of leather- and latex-clad sex club patrons (both gay and straight).

For over thirty years, drug dealers, addicts, transsexual prostitutes, and their johns peppered the neighborhood. The triangle building on the corner of 9th Avenue and 14th Street (present location of the übertrendy Vento

Trattoria Italian restaurant) was home to a string of establishments known as "Pig Parlors"—bars with back rooms and dungeons, run by the mafia, in which an estimated 150 men per night engaged in anonymous sex. In the late 1960s the building was called *the Triangle*. In the '70s and '80s, simply *J's*.

When *J's* lost its liquor license, the owners changed the name to *J's Hangout* and reopened it as a BYOB after hours club, which it remained until August of 2002, when the NYC Department of Health finally closed it down for good for promoting unsafe sex. Other sex clubs in the district included *Alex in Wonderland* (West Street at West 13th), with a bondage dungeon called *As*trick*, complete with slings and jail cells, occupying the basement; *the Anvil*, located in the still-thriving Liberty Inn Hotel at 51 10th Ave; *Hellfire* (also located in the Triangle Building), which catered to straight crowds. The members-only *Mineshaft*, the most infamous sex club in the history of the city (some might argue anywhere), was located at 835 Washington Street on the corner of Little West 12th, present home of the new Highline Restaurant & Bar.

With the exception of the heterosexual *Hogs & Heifers* (859 Washington), which successfully made the conversion from seedy sex den to trendy Manhattan dive bar, the clubs are all gone now. But if you look hard enough, up in the sky across the highway as you ride past, you can still find the sex.

Straddled above the Highline at West 13th Street, caddy corner from Pier 54 on the Greenway (the pier where the Carpathia steamship safely landed the rescued survivors of the Titanic), looms the Standard—the neighborhood's new '70s-era-style luxury hotel. Opened at the close of 2008, each of the Standard's 337 rooms comes with full-length, floor-to-ceiling windows, offering unparalleled views of the Hudson River and the Manhattan skyline. The most sought-after views, however, often come from visitors looking in—hotel management and staff openly encourage its guests to exhibit themselves as if behind the glass of an opulent multi-level peepshow—on public displays of nudity and sex. If you are enjoying this ride with young children, now might be a good time to direct their attention away from the Standard to the steel arched entrance of Pier

54, and share with them instead the tragic story of the Titanic and its 705 survivors; otherwise, look up, up, up in the sky to catch a nod *in flagrante* to yet another of the city's vanishing landscapes.

After the Standard and Pier 54, continue on past Chelsea Piers and the iceberg-looking building across the street. The massive sports and entertainment complex to your left is actually the marriage of four restored historic piers and their head houses. Pier 59 (where the Titanic was scheduled to dock before it sank off the coast of Newfoundland), along with piers 60–62, served as luxury liner slips and docking terminals during the city's heyday as the largest shipping port in the world.

In addition to the year-round multitiered golf driving range that now occupies Pier 59, the complex is home to two indoor ice skating rinks, a basketball court, swimming pool, gymnastics facility, batting cages, and just about any sport you can imagine except for maybe cricket. The twisted, frosted glass building across the street from it is the new Barry Diller building (Home Shopping Network and Expedia.com guru), designed by Canadian-born architect Frank Gehry, creator of the Dancing House in Prague and the Guggenheim Museum in Bilbao, Spain. If you are in need of a restroom, there are clean public facilities located at the north end of the piers. Be careful as you round the turn, though; this area is often congested with pedestrians, joggers, and rollerbladers crossing the path, as well as cars and taxis leaving the parking lot next door.

When you reach the Bike and Roll bike shop and the Intrepid Sea-Air-Space Museum, continue along the Greenway past West 46th Street and the west-side neighborhood known as Hell's Kitchen, whose name—the most common story goes—was coined by a 19th-century police officer named Dutch Fred the Cop. According to legend, Dutch Fred, a veteran on the force, was patrolling a particularly *hellish* section of the violent Irish immigrant district that stretched from 34th Street to 57th Street, from 8th Avenue to the Hudson River when a riot broke out. Standing there at the corner of West 39th and 10th Avenue, watching the mayhem, the rooky cop partnered with Fred marveled, "This place is hell itself." To which Dutch Fred responded, "Hell's a mild climate. This is

Hell's Kitchen." While the anecdote makes for a good story, a fun urban myth to regale friends with at parties, no documentation survives to suggest that a beat cop named Dutch Fred ever existed, let alone christened the infamous slum that birthed the notorious gangsters Owney "the Killer" Madden and Mickey Spillane—who liked to kidnap local merchants, beat them, then ransom them back to their families. Just as likely, among the many explanations given, the moniker of the neighborhood that inspired the Tony and Oscar award–winning musical *West Side Story* was born of the deplorable living conditions in the disease-ridden shanties and tenement hovels that housed the poor Irish dock workers here. Conditions which during the mid-nineteenth century were arguably worse than hell.

Either way, when the name first appeared in print in the *New York-Times* newspaper back in 1881, it fit and it stuck. A hundred and thirty years later, the gangs have gone, and with restored restaurant and theater rows on 46th and 42nd streets, the easternmost blocks have been wrapped into Times Square as a popular tourist destination.

As has become commonplace here, save a few old buildings, little of the old neighborhood is left. For years, real estate brokers have tried unsuccessfully to rename Hell's Kitchen "Clinton," so don't be confused if you hear the term. The just over one-mile-square area (2.4 km) is one of the few neighborhoods in Manhattan still considered somewhat affordable. Over the years, historically lower rents and close proximity to the Theater District have solidified Hell's Kitchen as home to the city's acting community. In addition to the Windermere (the second-oldest large apartment house in Manhattan; 129 E. 17th Street is considered the oldest), Hell's Kitchen houses the Actor's Studio and the Manhattan Plaza, a two-tower, forty-six-story federally-subsidized apartment building with 70 percent of its rental units reserved for performing artists. Noted residents have included cocreator and producer of the TV series *Seinfeld* and comedian, Kenny Kramer (the neighbor on which the character Kramer was based).

As you approach Pier 99 and the Department of Sanitation Marine Transfer Station at West 59th Street, veer left along the water, pass the railroad ruins, where you will see the backdrop of West New York in New Jersey and the Palisades across the river. Forging up out of the water like cloisters of petrified wood, the rusting trellis and float bridge to your left are the fossilized relics of the New York Central Railroad.

From 1900 to 1968, the NYC(R) was a major U.S. rail service, with a dense webbing of track stretching as far north as Canada, and west to Illinois. Pioneering technology at the turn of the twentieth century, the float bridge allowed for the transfer of freight cars to "connecting" barges (whose deck height was dependent on the level of the tide), without the risk of the cars falling into the river.

Enter Riverside Park at 72nd Street. If needed, public restrooms are located just a few blocks ahead at the playground. Conceptually designed by Frederick Law Olmsted, designer of Central Park, in the early 1870s, then redesigned sixty years later by "master builder" and Parks Commissioner Robert Moses to cover the railway, the first incarnation of the waterfront park was completed in 1910. Follow along the path to the 79th Street Boat Basin and the overlooking Boat Basin Café across from it above. Constructed in 1937, as part of Commissioner Moses's park and boardwalk expansion, the Boat Basin provides 116 slips at which year-round and seasonal boaters may dock their vessels.

Hungry? Grab a burger at the café and sit outside and watch the sailboats and cyclists, the colors turning on the leaves overhead, unable to believe you are smack in the heart of New York City. Or, if you can wait, ride up into the park then back down to the water just past 125th Street and Harlem and choose between a "Swag Sampler" from Dinosaur Bar-B-Que (visible from the path at 131st and 12th Avenue) and a healthier snack just up ahead at the outdoor fruit and produce section at the Fairway Market and deli at 132nd.

At the Wastewater Treatment Plant at 135th Street, jog around to the right, under the overpass, then left before the train tracks back onto the path. (This jog is a bit tricky. If you wind up at a dead end in front of

the Treatment Plant, you've missed it, and will need to double back ten or fifteen yards. Look for the little round NYC Greenway signs marking the route.) Once back on the path, veer to the left again around the fenced-in parking lot, and the staircase and elevator leading up to **Riverbank State Park,** a twenty-eight-acre, indoor/outdoor, multilevel, multiuse olive branch to the leaders and residents of Harlem.

Built on the roof of the Wastewater Treatment Plant, Riverbank Park is one of the city's more costly *mea culpa* endeavors. The one-and-a-half-million-dollar sewage processing center was plopped down on nine blocks of the neglected neighborhood's waterfront. So remember: If you choose to stop and hop on the elevator or climb the stairs to experience the park's storybook cliff-side views of Edgewater and the Palisades, don't drink the water. Also the NO BICYCLING! signs posted here are strictly enforced.

Continue along the Greenway and the brackish swells of the Hudson, lapping at the bank of wet glistening rocks dressing the shore like sequins on a ball gown, and weave around to the behemoth George Washington Bridge, rising up in the distance above the kaleidoscope-colored tree line.

At 155th Street, the Greenway enters Fort Washington Park and the upper Manhattan neighborhood of Washington Heights. The former Revolutionary War site and park is a favorite haunt of local fishermen.

You'll see rods dot the riverbank like needles in pincushions, reel seats wedged into the sediment between the rocks, lines taught, cast into the river like tightrope rigging. Traces of sea salt paint the air as these urban outdoorsmen tend to their reels, smoke, and joke with each other in varying dialects of Spanish, the dominant language spoken here.

After the fishermen, ride past the tennis courts toward the George Washington Bridge. Bathrooms are available at 165th and 170th streets. Stop for a moment and rest, or snack at the Little Red Lighthouse at the base of the bridge, officially called the Jeffrey's Hook Lighthouse, after the geographical point on which the little tower is erected.

Famous throughout the world as the title character in Hildegarde H. Swift's 1942 picture book, *The Little Red Lighthouse and the Great Gray Bridge,* is the story of the diminutive lighthouse's fear of becoming obsolete in the monstrous shadow of the big buff bridge towering above. Illustrated by Lynd Ward, the quaint tale reminds us that at the end of the day small things contribute just as great as tall. Sixteen years after it opened, the Great Gray Bridge (or the GW as it's locally known) put the Jeffrey's Hook Lighthouse out of business, and in 1947, the lighthouse was deemed no longer necessary. When a 1951 plan to tear it down sparked public protest, particularly among Swift fans, the parks and recreation department preserved the little red ships' beacon as a city landmark, eventually having

it listed on the *National Register of Historic Places* (for guided tour information and festivals, please call 212-304-2365).

Time to make your way up to the museum. **From the lighthouse, or if you choose not to stop and rest (which might not be a bad idea given the grades of the back-to-back hills ahead, as taking them from a dead stop promises to be painful),**

climb the path up to the right past the base of the bridge tower under the bridge. There is a reason the Continental Army built the fort from which Washington's troops—under the command of General Nathanael Greene—would defend New York against the British on the tract of land spanning what is now 155th Street to Dyckman Street in Inwood. As the highest natural point on the island, for miles Greene could see red coats coming from all directions. Little good it did; Greene's regiment was devastated in the 1776 Battle of Fort Washington. With the help from the Germans, in a three-pronged attack the British dispersed Washington's beleaguered army in a matter of hours, leaving 155 dead or injured, and 2,838 out of a total of 3,000 taken prisoner, of which only 800 survived to be released at the British surrender.

Continue to climb up to the right over the wooden footbridge into the tunnel and prepare for the second hill. This stage of the ride puts to rest the myth that New York is flat. Look around you a moment. Down at the water. Across to the Palisades. Listen for the trickle of the hundreds of natural streams and tributaries that drained once into the world's finest estuary below. Imagine riding this path back in 1609—on a mountain bike, of course, over dirt and rock instead of asphalt—before Henry Hudson made his ill-fated voyage.

The *Lenape* Indian word *Mannahatta*, from which this borough takes its name, means the "island of many hills." Prior to the Revolutionary War, Manhattan was still layered with some five hundred jagged hill and rock formations lined with forests of over seventy species of trees where birds and other forms of wildlife abounded. But by the mid nineteenth century, under the leadership and guidance of DeWitt Clinton, longtime New York mayor, governor, and visionary, we bulldozed it. The whole island. Except for a couple of stubborn patches here and there (like Morningside and Washington Heights), the island was flattened to make way for the new, 1811, Manhattan Grid—a predesigned schematic encompassing twenty-three square miles (59.5 km²) of concrete real estate and the two million plus people (at its peak) who would squeeze themselves into it.

Do not be embarrassed if you have to get off and walk here. If you are on a single speed, or fixed gear, you most likely will. Bike NYC did. (Don't tell anybody though. It's on the down low yo.) **Once you reach the top and are again on fairly level ground, ride along the West Side Highway toward the pedestrian ramp and walkway at 181st Street.** The graffiti-peppered containing wall to your right is haunted by a ghost of

another bygone era. Not too long ago, during the 1970s and '80s, New York boasted a thriving graffiti culture that was largely forced dormant under the mayoral administrations of Edward I. Koch and Rudolph Giuliani. The jury remains hung on what, if anything, the pastime contributed to the city's ongoing conversation on culture and art. The answers are as varied as the individuals who might provide them. Some flat out consider it vandalism. Others, specifically some of the old subway car tags, belong on permanent display in a museum somewhere. The crews themselves, hard to say. Some of the younger generations, starting out at the time all went quiet, saw it as a way to reclaim the public and commercial spaces that had been taken from them, or made inaccessible from the start. Some just wanted to see their names up in lights. While others simply believed the world was their canvas, and since the world lives and breathes in New York City, where better to paint their masterpieces than on the public spaces where they would always be seen. Like the skyscraper kings before them, the John Jakob Raskobs, the Chryslers, and Van Allens they yearned to leave their mark on this city, and over the years grew more and more daring, writing their names across the highest reaches in the sky. Buildings, billboards, overpasses.

In 1988, the dynamic duo of brothers called SaneSmith made the city's most wanted list for "bombin'" the Brooklyn Bridge in response to the Koch subway car crackdown. Pretty soon, respect, or street credibility, was no longer given based solely on the craft and style of your tag, but on the difficulty of the acrobatics one had to perform to "get up" as it were. Climbing poles, balance beam walking across catwalks, standing on inches-wide ledges, or hanging from them by hand thirty feet above water or ground, earned "mad cred." In other words, in the end, like the real estate boom in this town, before the bust, as far as graffiti art was concerned, location, location, location was everything.

The containing wall to your right was once a piece of the canvas for a tagger whom many in the culture consider the king of New York graffiti writers: "JA," also known as bit part movie actor Jonathan Avildsen (he played the character "Snake" in the movie *Karate Kid III*). During his reign as graffiti king, JA was famous for the unbelievable places he had been able to get up. He was everywhere, and, it is rumored, he still wears the scars from the repeated beatings he received by the police to prove it. Since painted over, in the wee hours of a morning in 1995, JA was arrested while bombing his tag across the crown of this wall. Later that same night, legend has it, in a paradigmatic display of the kind of stubborn grit and resolve it took to build this city, after he was arrested, processed, fingerprinted, and released, Avildsen returned to the scene with a second ladder (the first one was confiscated), freshly "racked" cans of spray paint and finished the job.

Entering Fort Tryon Park

From the pedestrian ramp and walkway, you have two options for arriving at the Cloisters.

Option #1: If you prefer to cycle in, climb the ramp and use the pedestrian bridge to cross the West Side Highway. Turn right when you come off the bridge onto Riverside Drive. Riverside Drive is one-way here, so for safety reasons you'll want to ride on the sidewalk. The first street you come to, Plaza Lafayette (181st Street), turn left. **(Please note: The road becomes a little bumpy here, and can be very busy during peak times of**

day.) Follow Plaza Lafayette to the corner and jog left, then right onto 181st Street. Stay on 181st for three blocks, passing Cabrini Boulevard and Pinehurst Avenue (on your right only), before turning left into the bike lane on Fort Washington Avenue. **You are almost there!** Follow the bike path on Fort Washington all the way to the entrance to Fort Tryon (approximately ten blocks, just past 190th Street), around the park to the museum. **(Remain alert here! Although there is a bike lane, traffic is dense and, unfortunately, the lane is often used by cars as a parking lot.)**

Option #2: If you would rather stay on the Greenway a little longer and don't mind hauling your bike down a flight of stairs and walking into the park, pass the pedestrian ramp and bridge and follow the protected path until it dead-ends at a concrete staircase (the path narrows to single file in a couple of places here, so be on the lookout for oncoming cyclists). Descend the staircase and walk your bike along the sidewalk under the overpass past the entrance to New York State Route 9A, then jump back on your wheels and turn left onto Staff Street and ride down the hill. At Dyckman Street, the bottom of the hill, turn right into the bike lane. Stay on Dyckman for two blocks, turning right a second time at Payson Avenue **(if for any reason you are in need of a bike shop at this point, Tread Bike Shop is less than a block away at 250 Dyckman).** At the end of Payson Avenue, cross Riverside Drive, hop off your bike and walk into the park. Follow the footpath around Fort Tryon until you reach the museum.

Welcome to the Cloisters!

Returning

As with entering, you have a couple of options when leaving Fort Tryon to return to the starting point.

Option #1: Exit the park via the bike lane, ride back down Fort Washington Avenue to 181st Street and hang a right back to the pedestrian bridge and Greenway to return the way you came.

Option #2: If you are game, explore the Washington Heights neighborhood a bit, instead, and drop back to the Greenway a little farther down at 138th Street at Riverbank State Park.

To explore Washington Heights, exit the park via the bike lane as in option #1, and ride down Fort Washington Avenue until it curves around to Broadway at West 159th Street. In addition to the Cloisters and the mouthwatering food to be found here, Washington Heights is home to a number of historical landmarks and monuments as well as residents who have made considerable contributions to American culture and society. Audubon Terrace, a truss of five neoclassical beaux arts buildings named after "bird" artist and naturalist John James Audubon at 155th Street, houses the Hispanic Society of America—a museum dedicated to the preservation of Spanish, Portuguese, and Latino art and culture, boasting extensive collections of Francisco Goya and the artist formerly known as El Greco. Dating back to pre–Revolutionary War, on the edge of Highbridge Park, stands the Morris-Jumel Mansion, the oldest house in Manhattan. Also located along Highbridge Park is the building simply known as 555 Edgecombe Avenue, listed on the National Register of Historic Places as the home of noted African American actor and spirituals singer Paul Robeson, bandleader and jazz pioneer Count Basie, and boxing legend Joe Louis.

Beginning in the early 1900s, not long after Ellis Island replaced Castle Clinton as the emigration depot, Washington Heights became a haven for various immigrants fleeing one type of tyranny or another. Escaping the increasingly crowded and slumlike conditions to which they were relegated downtown (by 1900 the city's population neared four million), the newly arrived Irish began to settle here first. After the Irish, during the 1930s and '40s, European Jews fled to the Heights to escape Nazism. In the '50s and '60s, it was the Greeks, followed by Cubans and Puerto Ricans, and by the 1980s the area had turned solidly Dominican, which it remains today along with a smattering of other Spanish-speaking nationals such as Ecuadorians and Mexicans.

At Broadway, turn right and "bomb" down the only street in Manhattan that runs the entire length of the island without interruption. Pass the Church of the Intercession at 155th Street and the Trinity Cemetery, the borough's only active burial ground. At 145th Street, turn right, and drop down to Riverside Drive. Here again, you

have a couple of options. You can walk your bike across the 145th Street pedestrian bridge into Riverbank State Park and take the stairs or the escalator down to the Greenway. Or, you can turn left and follow Riverside Drive to 138th Street, where you'll jog right, then left, skirting the entrance to the park, and drop down to Twelfth Avenue. Follow the NYC Greenway signs back to the path and return the way you came.

(While this ride takes you from Battery Park to the Cloisters and back, it can be started or completed at any point on the Greenway.)

On The	**NAME: TALIAH LEMPERT**
	AGE: 42
	OCCUPATION: ARTIST/PAINTER
Wheel	**RIDE: BIANCHI 80'S ROAD BIKE (AMONG OTHERS)**

CHAPTER 2

THE CEMETERY BELT

(Eighteen Miles)

BOROUGH OF THE DEAD

Visible from space, the Cemetery Belt is the child of a nineteenth-century marriage of laws passed by the New York State Legislature and the Common Council of New York City. The first, the Rural Cemetery Act, approved by the legislature in 1847, allowed nonprofit organizations (i.e., churches and synagogues) to purchase tax-exempt, undeveloped countryside for sale to New Yorkers as burial plots. Prior to 1847, The City's deceased were mostly laid to rest in churchyards, or on private farms and estates, with the unknown, criminal, and indigent arranged side by side and one on top of the other in large public trenches called potter's fields—the name, a reference to a verse in the Gospel of Matthew in the Bible. But as Manhattan's population swelled from three hundred thousand in the 1840s to almost two million by the turn of the century (in part due to the waves of immigrants fleeing famine in Ireland), real estate became much too precious a commodity to squander away on the dead. Although the state prohibited these organizations from owning more than 250 acres in any one county, religious sects and land speculators sidestepped this restriction by acquiring property that sat astride county lines, particularly the line between Brooklyn and Queens.

The husband law to this act was enacted five years later. Fearing that the scores of bodies from back-to-back decades with cholera epidemics squatting in The City's potter's fields were causing the disease to leach into the drinking water, coupled with the desire to reclaim valuable real estate, in 1852, the Common Council ordered a permanent embargo on interments on the island of Manhattan. The ban not only applied to future burials, but thousands of those long underground were exhumed and booted to

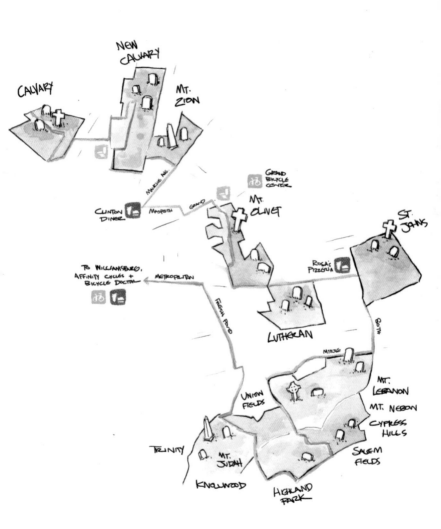

CALVARY

NEW CALVARY

MT. ZION

CLINTON DINER

MASPETH

GRAND

GRAND BICYCLE CENTER

MT. OLIVET

ST. JOHNS

ROSA'S PIZZERIA

TO WILLIAMSBURG, AFFINITY CYCLES + BICYCLE DOCTOR

METROPOLITAN

FRESH POND

LUTHERAN

80TH

MYRTLE

MT. LEBANON

MT. NEBOH

CYPRESS HILLS

UNION FIELDS

SALEM FIELDS

TRINITY

MT. JUDAH

KNOLLWOOD

HIGHLAND PARK

the outer boroughs as well. Together the laws gave birth to a frenzied and prudent land grab of the hills and farms and ponds peppered along the sparsely populated western Queens border (the 1840 census counting only fourteen thousand residents at the time), spawning in turn a nine-mile swath of headstones, mausoleums, crypts, monuments, and memorials that could arguably be called the father of the modern-day death industry. From Blissville to Ridgewood, tens of millions of New Yorkers are buried here, the rich often on manicured hillsides, shaded by fir trees, with eternal postcard views of Manhattan. Though most are as cramped and crowded in death as we live in life in this city, packed into twenty-three separate cemeteries buttressed against each other, winding and snaking through the boroughs like segments of a giant centipede. From legendary escape artist Harry Houdini, notorious gangster Lucky Luciano, and Hollywood bad girl Mae West to the unnamed and unsung, whose lives and names, chiseled in ancient scripts foreign to most eyes, have been all but forgotten.

If you were born here, or in one of the nearby counties, or adjacent northeastern states, chances are you have relatives buried in one of these cemeteries—Calvary, Cypress Hills, Mt. Olivet, Machpelah. A grandparent, or great-grandparent entombed in Mount Zion. Distant Old World cousins resting in Lutheran, or All Souls. The full-circle exit depot for the steady stream of immigrants who, from 1855 to 1954, washed up on these shores to begin a new life, to make a better way for themselves and their children, where the names we might find etched in the slabs of weather-worn granite match those scrawled in the annals of Ellis Island.

The Ride

Start at the entrance to Calvary Cemetery in the borough of Queens, at the intersection of Greenpoint and Gale avenues in Bliss-ville—a pizza slice of a neighborhood nearly forgotten, wedged into the southern rim of Long Island City, between the Long Island Expressway and Newtown Creek, a tributary of the East River. Purchased in 1837, by Robert Fulton apprentice and steam engine developer Neziah Bliss, who also settled much of neighboring Greenpoint, Blissville floundered as little more than an outpost until 1848, when the trustees of Saint Patrick's Cathedral opened the gates to Calvary. Within months, new and old industries sprouted to life to accommodate the bereaved who traveled from Manhattan by ferry and stagecoach—later

by rail, once the Greenpoint Avenue line was constructed—to bury their dead. From monument works, to tombstone engravers, hotels, saloons in which to wash down sorrows and roadside florists, Blissville was soon the aptly named gangway from which deceased New Yorkers embarked on the afterlife. Though Calvary remains one of the largest and oldest cemeteries in the country (over three million people are buried in New Calvary alone), today, much of the original Blissville, including its de facto claim to fame as the causeway to the great hereafter, has been painted over. In its place, a lone residential block of one- and two-story pre-WWII era single family homes absorbed into Long Island City, sandwiched on all sides by a graffiti-tagged mash-up of auto repair and body shops, self-storage warehouses, motels, and truck rental companies. Even the streets have been renamed. Review Avenue replacing B Street. Bradley and Gale avenues, D and E streets. Yet if we look close enough, beneath the surface, haunts of the old neighborhood still hover. Under the Blissville Deli & Grocery, for example, housed on the corner of Bradley Avenue and 35th Street, is a building constructed back in 1901. Or the Best Western City View Inn, the old PS 80 schoolhouse, also built at the turn of the century, on Greenpoint Avenue, converted after the Second World War into an Orthodox Jewish seminary by a community of Satmar Hasidim, then, after standing vacant for thirty years, and rumored to be haunted, a string of failed motor inns until the late 1980s, when it was purchased by the Best Western Hotels corporation. The Bantry Bay Publick House on the corner of Greenpoint and Bradley is the location of another Blissville phantom. Known for its burgers and shepherd's pie, the Irish-themed pub and restaurant site was once home to the Bradley Inn—a nineteenth-century hotel and tavern catering to travelers and cemetery goers. In addition to serving up mouthwatering meals and drink, the pub also serves as the official headquarters of the New York City Cork Association (as in the County Cork, in Ireland), whose club origins date back to 1884.

Ride through the gates past the Queen Anne–style gatehouse into the cemetery. On land obtained in 1845 from the Alsop family, Calvary was one of the first cemeteries established after passage of the Rural Cemetery Act. Forty hectares of farmland at the time of purchase, with the acquisition of New Calvary (also known as Second, Third, and Fourth Calvaries) later in the century, the cemetery now encompasses an unrivaled 365 acres (or 400 football fields) of tombstones. In addition to the fictional character Don Corleone (Section 1 West), a number of real-life New York mobsters are buried there. Among them, Little Augie Pisano (Section 47, DeSalvo Mausoleum), a ranking member of the Genovese crime family, christened at birth as Anthony Carfano; Frankie Marlow (Section 47, plot 64), of the Joe "the Boss" Masseria family, born Gandolfo Curto; and Ignatius Saietta—the brutal Lupo the Wolf (Section 35, Ciro Terranova plot), a merciless Black Hand extortionist who terrorized Little Italy by strangling to death anyone who failed to pay up, then burning their corpses in a horse stable up in East Harlem.

Continue riding along St. John's Avenue. Interred in section 9, plot 443, is alleged Brooklyn Bridge jumper Steve Brodie. On July 23, 1886, three years after the bridge was completed, and only fourteen months after swim-coach-turned-daredevil Robert E. Odlum plunged to his death attempting the same feat, small-time Bowery bookie Brodie garnered overnight fame when he claimed to have hung from the girders and dropped 120 feet into the rushing East River. A diminutive man, appear-

ing not much older than a schoolboy, just four seconds after he struck the water and disappeared under the currents, Brodie surfaced not only alive, but completely unscathed. Not a single scratch or complaint, other than a pain in his side caused, according to his wife, by an old unrelated prejump injury. He did it, said the bookie, to collect on a $200 bet.

Though the death-defying leap (some have called it insane) made headlines across the city, in light of Robert Odlum's recent fate, many met Brodie's claim with skepticism. First rumored, then inked into legend as fact, the fabled jump is now dismissed as a hoax. It is widely held that Brodie was never on the bridge to begin with. Instead, he hid under a pier below, while a friend drove a dummy onto the cable-suspended roadway above and threw it over the railing in Brodie's place. When the dummy splashed into the water, Brodie swam out from hiding to wait for the rescue boats. As soon as he was ferried ashore, he was arrested. Hoax or no, newspaper coverage of the stunt hoisted the little known gambler atop the city's shoulders and crowned him hero. Brodie wasted no time parlaying his new celebrity status into a successful venture as a popular saloon owner on the Bowery, where the retelling and no doubt embellishing of his dubious story was the main attraction. Thirty years after he died, Hollywood filmmaker Raoul Walsh further immortalized Brodie's deception in the 1933 movie *The Bowery* and the term "taking" or "pulling a Brodie" has since been folded into the city's modern-day slang lexicon, meaning to attempt or commit suicide by jumping off a bridge, or to perpetrate a dangerous and idiotic stunt.

At the intersection of St. John's and St. Mary's avenues, the end of Sections 7 and 8, you have a couple of options for continuing. But first,

look behind you, and drink in the audacity of Manhattan. The mooring station for dirigibles that never worked atop the Empire State Building, punctuating the skyline. The Chrysler spire—for eleven brief months, from 1930–31, the tallest building in the world. The Trump Tower and Citicorp wedge.

If you want to view the site where Vito Corleone was buried in *The Godfather,* cross St. Mary's Avenue past section marker 1 West to your left and drop down the hill toward the Johnston Mausoleum in Section 6—the opulent chamber high up on a rise that looks more like the shrine or palace of an ancient king rather than the burial place of a department store owner and dry goods dealer. Encircled down below by a moat of hobbitlike crypts and vaults, the massive tomb and chapel was erected at a cost of $100,000 in the late 1800s by a man named John Johnston—a poor Irish immigrant who worked his way through the mercantile trade from rags to riches then back to rags again, when just a few short years after his death, his younger brother, Robert, frittered away the family fortune.

Follow the road to the left of the mausoleum and stop in front of the Hildreth and Gary vaults on your right and look to the bank of headstones opposite. A prop constructed solely for the film, then immediately dismantled after production, the Vito Corleone monument stood just a few feet back and to the right of the Daly grave. Reportedly, and somewhat ironic in a life-imitates-art sort of way, with 150 extras, twenty limousines, and $12,000 in floral arrangements, the staging of Don Corleone's fake funeral rivaled the cost of John Johnston's real one.

Continue around to the right behind the Johnston Mausoleum and up the hill to Calvary Avenue. Turn right when you reach the intersection. Follow Calvary across the cemetery along the BQE and the Kosciuszko Bridge to your left (the former site of the old Penny Bridge, named after the cost of the toll charged to cross it) and head for the rear gate exit. (To bypass the Corleone funeral site: from St. John's Avenue, instead of crossing St. Mary's, turn right and either climb the slight hill to circle around the chapel, or hang your first left across Central Avenue and drop down to the rear gate.) Either way will take you past Section 4, the site of the Alsop family plots. A boneyard fenced within a boneyard, as part of the purchase price for the Alsop farm, the trustees of St. Patrick's Cathedral promised to maintain and care for the family's burial ground as it would the rest of the gravesites. The Alsop tombs date back as far as 1712, and mark the only Protestant remains known to lie in a Catholic cemetery.

Pedal through the exit gate and turn left onto Review Avenue, doubling back along the cemetery up the hill toward the Long Island Expressway. Follow Review as it turns into Laurel Hill Boulevard, wrapping under the expressway onto 54th road into a quick jog left then right onto 53rd Avenue via 43rd Street. The hill you are power-

ing up, or struggling with (it's fairly steep), as well as the land smothered beneath the homage to industry around you, used to be coated with laurel trees. Hence the name of the neighborhood Laurel Hill, the pinch of single-family homes sprinkled about is all that remains of the nineteenth-century residential community that once thrived here.

At the light at 53rd Avenue and 48th Street, turn left onto 48th and pass under the LIE, then right at Laurel Hill Boulevard and ride up onto the sidewalk. (In general, it is against the law to bike on the sidewalk in New York, but in cases such as this where there is minimal pedestrian traffic and safety is a concern, it is acceptable.) The florist in front of you, O'laughlin's, has sold flowers and graveside mementos on this doorstep to New Calvary for 118 years now. Riley Brothers Monuments, the stone brick building next door, with the unmarked slabs of granite tossed about the yard, is the oldest business on the corner, dating back to 1882. The neighborhood, in case you are wondering, is Woodside—from its birth in 1869, home to the largest enclave of Irish Americans in the borough of Queens.

On the sidewalk, ride toward 58th Street along the cobblestone retaining wall shadowing Laurel Hill Boulevard under the BQE, parting the sea of gravestones that make up New Calvary Cemetery—splayed behind the retaining wall and the wrought iron fence across the street from you. The limestone and granite markers in the cemetery are not the only memorials raised along this trenchlike stretch of the boulevard. Midway between O'laughlin's and the entrance gates to the cemetery, you'll notice one of the BQE support columns to your left has been clothed in offerings of hearts and roses. Flowers and mementos, purchased no doubt from O'laughlin's, a sleeve of the words "R.I.P. Eric, Pedro and Tommy" tattooed on all sides the length of the pillar. The altar in front of you honors three Queens locals slain on impact when the driver of the car in which they were speeding lost control and crashed into the column. They were twenty-six and twenty-seven years old. Their names were Pedro Sanchez, Tommy J. Owens, and Eric Saguenette. The car they were pried from looked as though something wild had taken hold of it and wrenched it indistinguishable. Police at the scene said they never had a chance.

At the gate to 2nd Calvary, turn right into the cemetery. (If you reach the light at 58th Street, you've gone too far, and will need to turn around and double back.) Ride through 2nd Calvary and pedal around the "Rachel Weeping for Her Children" memorial between Sections 11 and 12 toward the tunnel under Borden Avenue and the LIE ahead. Two sections to your left, Jamaican-born Harlem Renaissance poet, journalist, and novelist Claude McKay is buried in tomb 42-14-R-5. Author of *Harlem Shadows* and the autobiographical *A Long Way from Home*, McKay was considered a radical because he used his pen and talent to urge African Americans to demand and fight for their freedoms and equality. Today we might call him a community organizer.

Drop through the tunnel and curve around to the right up the slight hill onto St. Matthew's Avenue. Follow St. Matthew's a short distance to the exit gate at 50th Street. (If needed, bathroom facilities are located just before the exit on your right.) Exit the cemetery and turn left onto 50th Street, then left again at the corner onto 55th Avenue at

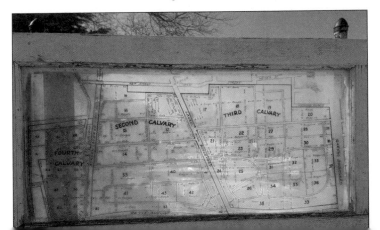

the Duane Reade Warehouse. Follow 55th Avenue to 58th Street and turn left back toward the LIE. At the intersection of Borden and 58th, veer right across Borden onto the sidewalk plaza beneath the LIE, then turn right again onto the 54th Avenue sidewalk across the street. (This is a tricky intersection. Be sure to wait for the green light and remain alert, as cars are both entering and exiting the Long Island Expressway.) Follow the 54th Avenue sidewalk along Mount Zion Cemetery until 54th Avenue becomes a two-way road, then ride on the street toward the entrance to Mount Zion and Maurice Avenue.

On a seventy-eight-acre parcel of land in Maspeth, the oldest European settlement in Queens (dating back to 1642), 210,000 headstones bank down the slope of a rise shadowed by the smokestacks of the Betts Avenue Incinerator in the Department of Sanitation's refuse lot next door. Mount Zion Cemetery has been laying the city's Jewry to rest on this parcel of land since 1893, the inactive smokestacks rising up in the background, a chilling reminder of unconscionable events past. As with all the cemeteries in this belt, like the city itself, young and old are buried here, famous and unknown, clustered

together in orderly charnel villages called lodges and societies, many with locketlike images of the deceased emblazoned into their headstones. From rabbis to lyricists to factory workers, including Rose Rosenfeld Freedman (Path 31R, Gate 10, Czernowitzer Bukowiner Lodge), who was the last living survivor of the Triangle Shirtwaist—the devastating 1911 catastrophe that consumed the lives of 146 garment workers and injured scores more.

At 4:45 PM, the afternoon of March 25, 1911, the Triangle Shirtwaist Factory—a garment industry sweatshop specializing in ladies blouses housed on the top three floors of the Asch Building on the corner of Washington Place and Greene streets in Manhattan—caught fire. Though never confirmed, the reigning culprit was believed to be a smoldering cigarette butt, or match tossed unawares into a scrap bin aided by shirtwaist cuttings helter-skelter about the floor. Within minutes all three floors were engulfed in smoke and flames. What left a particularly heinous glow on the Triangle fire was that no one was held responsible. Although the owners were charged with manslaughter, they were acquitted. The only good to come from the fire was a host of new labor welfare laws. Reports later read that the girls were essentially trapped: with one escape route slowed by a turnstyle, while the other escape routes had been bolted shut by management to prevent cutters from sneaking cigarette breaks in the stairwell. When fire blocked access to the Greene Street exit, rather than be burned alive, many of the women ran to the windows and jumped in desperation. Sixty-two to be exact, all to their deaths, wave after wave of them, mistaken at first for bundles of fabric tossed to the street by the unsavory owners in an attempt to salvage some of the inventory. For several uncomprehending minutes that felt like hours, on a warm and sunny spring day in Manhattan, the sky seemed to be raining down bodies in a bit of eerie

Dickensian foreshadowing to a similar sunny day rain ninety years in the future. Before the attacks on the World Trade Center on September 11, 2001, the Triangle Shirtwaist Fire was the worst workplace tragedy in The City's history.

Rose Rosenfeld escaped, along with a handful of others, by climbing a smoldering staircase to the abandoned executive floor above, then braving another smoke-filled stairway to the roof, where firemen ferried her to the safe harbor of the roof next door. As one of fewer than one hundred survivors from the nineth floor, the portrait of the Austrian immigrant's postfire years—as eulogized in her obituary—paints the picture of a woman determined to taste as much of life as life had to serve. By the time she was laid to rest in Mount Zion, at the age of 107, Rose had graduated college, married, and raised three children. She was a lifelong advocate and spokesperson for labor law reform, returned to college at the age of fifty-nine to earn a business degree, lied about her age and was hired on to an insurance company in the accounting department at sixty-four, had mastered seven languages, and was still enrolled in Spanish classes until the day she died. Featured in the 2000 PBS documentary *The Living Century,* of turning 106, Rose remarked that the age was merely "a number. I lived that long," she said, "not only on account of my genes, but on account of my attitude."

Spoken like a true New Yorker, Rose.

Other interments worth noting here are lyricist Lorenz Hart (Path 8R), of the Rogers and Hart Broadway songwriting team, who penned the lyrics to *My Funny Valentine* and *The Lady Is a Tramp,* among numerous others, and novelist Nathaniel West (Path 27R, Daniel Webster Benevolent Society, Weinstein Plot), author of *Day of the Locusts.* **Restroom facilities are located just inside the main gate on your left as you exit.**

From the exit, turn left onto 54th Avenue, then right at the stop sign onto Maurice Avenue and cross back under the LIE. Follow Maurice past 55th Drive, 56th Avenue, and 56th Drive to Maspeth Avenue and turn left. If you are hungry, the Clinton Diner—just ahead in the triangle bordered by Maspeth and 57th Place and Rust Street—is a wonderful spot to enjoy a great cheap meal, or coffee and desert. Plus, in case you missed the opportunity back at Mount Zion or New Calvary, you can use the restroom while you are there.

Ranked the second-best truck stop in the country by the makers of Vivarin, caffeinated mental alertness pills, the Clinton Diner & Bar has been a favorite haunt for local and long haul truckers and just plain ol' locals since 1935. Classic diner fare here includes burgers (juicy half-pounders), with shakes and fries, chicken cutlets, meat loaf, London broil, omelets, pancakes. Pretty much what you would expect from an American diner, only really, *really* good. Oh, and did we mention cheap? If you experience déjà vu when you enter, and sense that you've been here before, chances are you remember the space age diner from one of the fifteen different movies that have been filmed here. From *Goodfellas* to *You Don't Know Jack.* Locals come here to view the memorabilia plastered all over the walls as much as they do for the food. **Pedal along Maspeth Avenue to 61st Street, through the blocks of one- and two-story row houses and single family homes (a number dating back to the 19th**

century), with simple cared-for front lawns and sidewalks lined with ash, maple and brindled trunk London plane. Turn right onto 61st Street past Three Sons Pizzeria and Italian Restaurant, then hang a left at Russo Bakery onto Grand Avenue. Follow Grand Avenue until it intersects with Maspeth, 64th Street, and Flushing (Maspeth turned one way the opposite direction at 61st, which is why we had you circle around). Bike NYC never encourages riding the wrong way down one-way streets as it is both unsafe and against the law. If you wish to take the risk on your own, however, this leg of the ride can be shortened a bit by taking Maspeth Avenue directly to Grand and Flushing. Follow the signs and execute the slight "jog around," turning left onto Flushing, which turns into Grand again in a little under one thousand feet (three hundred meters). Stay on Grand through the Maspeth business district until you reach Remsen Place (the florists shops on the block should signal the approach to Mount Olivet Cemetery). Turn right at Remsen into the main entrance off Grand. (If you're in need of a bike shop, Grand Bicycle Center is just up ahead at 70-13 Grand Avenue and 71st Street).

Aesthetically, with its meandering pathways and rolling hillsides nurtured by an arboretum of shade trees and far-off shimmering views of Manhattan, Mount Olivet is one of the more agreeable cemeteries you'll discover on this ride—in a handsome, well-mannered sort of way. Named

for a ridge of hills in the New Testament in the Bible, east of Jerusalem and blanketed with olive trees on the other side of the Jehoshaphat Valley, where Jesus went to pray in the Garden of Gethsemane the night he was betrayed by Judas, Mount Olivet, also known as the "Garden Cemetery" opened its gates in 1850, to serve the interment needs of The City's Episcopalian community. Soon, however, in

1851, the board repealed the religion requirement, and the cemetery has operated as a nonreligious, nonsectarian burial ground since. **Veer left at the cemetery office (on your right) onto Central Avenue.**

Like most cemeteries in New York, Mount Olivet has its share of notable interments. Among them, Georges Matchabelli, a former Russian prince who immigrated to New York after the Russian Revolution, with his wife, Princess Norina (notable in her own right as "the Madonna" in the London production of Max Reinhardt's *The Miracle).* As with most early immigrants to this country, regardless of former positions or training, the prince and princess had to learn to scrape by on more meager pursuits and incomes. Luckier than most, however, the couple was able to open and scratch out a living off a small antique shop on Madison Avenue before the prince, an amateur chemist, hit it big with his own perfume line: *Prince Matchabelli Perfumes,* sold in bottles designed by Norina topped with replicas of the Matchabelli family crown. Though no longer adorned with the royal seal (Norina sold the line after Georges passed away in 1936), Prince Matchabelli perfumes can still be found on fragrance counters.

Follow Central around past the Kwanzan cherry trees across Edgewood, Border, and Hope avenues. Continue climbing and wrapping around Central past the ash trees at the intersection with Hemlock Lane through a grove of Sugar Maples, White Pine, and Common Horsechestnuts, passing Clinton Avenue on your way to the Hillside Mausoleums opposite Ascension Road.

Most entombed here were plain old everyday New Yorkers, businessmen and women who did not become famous, yet made no less indelible a mark on those who knew them. Buried there are teachers and office workers who set up the grill and barbecued on sidewalks as soon as the weather broke, who as children splashed around in the geysers of busted fire hydrants in lieu of swimming pools. People like Sarah Strasheim Sandmeyer, a homemaker and housewife who raised two children, was grandmother to three more, then took a job sorting chocolate in a candy factory several years after they were grown. A lifelong member of the Order of the

Eastern Star (since 1850, the largest Mason fraternity in the world open to both men and women, including Eleanor Roosevelt, American Red Cross organizer Clara Barton, author Zora Neal Hurston, and poet, essayist, and novelist Maya Angelou), one of Sarah's favorite pastimes was going to the movies, and she made a point to attend them as often as she could.

At the Mausoleums, jog to the right then left onto St. James Avenue past the Greek Church and Sweet Gums on Child Pine Slope, then turn right onto Border Avenue. Follow Border to the exit and turn left on Mount Olivet Crescent. (If needed, restrooms are located just inside the gate.)

(Alternate Route: If the Grand Street gate is closed for some reason, during the cemetery's open hours, continue on Grand and turn right onto Borden Avenue, then right again onto 69th Street. Follow 69th to Elliot Avenue and hang another right. Be careful! The road narrows here and there isn't much of a shoulder. Climb the slight hill up Elliot between Mount Olivet on your right and All Faiths Cemetery sprawling into Lutheran on your left. Turn left at the top of the hill onto Mount Olivet Crescent.) **Follow Mt. Olivet Crescent south past All Faiths Cemetery to Metropolitan Avenue and turn right.** Incorporated in 1852, as Lutheran Cemetery, as its name implies, the cemetery was founded to provide inexpensive dignified burials to New Yorkers of limited means and those of all faiths. The name was changed from Lutheran to All Faiths in 1990. Over 500,000 New Yorkers are interred here. **Continue east on Metropolitan, formerly the Williamsburgh and Jamaica Turnpike, through Middle Village.** Settled by the English in the early 1800s, the area was christened Middle Village because it lay midway between the nineteenth-century townships of Williamsburgh, Brooklyn, and Jamaica, Queens. Another old neighborhood that blossomed with the dawn of the cemetery age, unlike Blissville, Middle Village has prospered into a healthy middle-class (no pun intended) community. The nearly two-hundred-year-old village is also the home of Anthony Casamassima, the former cemetery caretaker turned professional grave robber, arrested in a sting operation by the FBI for stealing a Tiffany's stained-glass window from a mausoleum

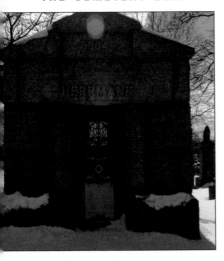

in a Middle Village cemetery, and peddling it to a Tiffany's expert for $60,000, who in turn was convicted of reselling it to a collector for over three and a half times the investment, knowing it was stolen. According to court records and a 1999 *New York Times* newspaper story, Mr. Casamassima said he was not so much stealing the eighty-some odd windows, pedestals, statues, busts, and cremation urns he pillaged, but "liberating" them from the dastardly clutches of future vandals and negligent caretakers. For fifteen years, from cemeteries throughout Middle Village and beyond, including the bone repositories on either side of you as well as the one toward which you are riding, Casamassima stole from the dead and sold to the rich, leaving Christmas wreaths in place of the plundered ornaments in a cross between some kind of Robinhood of the Damned and the Grinch.

Pedal through Middle Village on Metropolitan Avenue past Christ the King High School and the original Lutheran Cemetery into the business district. If you have yet to stop for something to eat, now would be a good time to sample true Queens pizza, with a "Grandma's" slice at Rosa's Pizzeria and Restaurant on the northwest corner of Metropolitan and 78th Street. You can also stock up on water while you're there, and make use of the facilities before heading toward St. John's, the cemetery just up ahead. Or, if it's Sunday and you're cool on water and electrolyte replacements, you might want to wait a few blocks until you hit the cemetery. On Sundays, the Pretzel Man sets up shop on the southeast corner of 80th street and Metropolitan, across from the entrance to the cemetery. Although this is a busy intersection, you can't miss him. To advertise his stand, he ties a giant inflated pretzel to the southeast corner traffic light, and a second one around the street lamp next to the stand. **After the pretzel stand, or should you decide to forgo it, you have a couple of options:**

Option 1: You can enter the gate to explore St. John's, established in 1879, and seek out the tombs of mob syndicate bad boys Lucky Luciano and John J. Gotti, or "culture wars" bad boy, controversial photographer Robert Mapplethorpe, whose homoerotic images of nude gay men and in-your-face self-portraits in which the artist documented his wasting to death from AIDS, so boiled the ire of conservatives in congress that, upon discovery that the nation's leading art patron—the National Endowment for the Arts (NEA)—funded a retrospective of Mapplethorpe's work, a few short months after the artist's death in 1989, the legislative body slashed the endowment's budget, forbidding it to fund any future homoerotic art projects, as well as a number of other categories the Republican-controlled congress deemed pornographic or offensive.

Option #2: If you wish to keep riding, and would rather bypass St. John's, **turn right onto 80th Street, heading south over the railroad bridge toward Myrtle Avenue. Make another right onto Myrtle at the Forest Park Golf Course and continue on Myrtle through Glendale to Cooper Avenue.** Founded in 1642, by the Reverend Francis Doughty under the charter of the Dutch West India Company, Glendale was originally called Fresh Ponds, for all the freshwater pools and marshes puddled over the landscape. Until the 1860s, when the area was officially renamed Glendale, Fresh Ponds was a prosperous German farming town, with what is now Myrtle Avenue—from 73rd Street to Cooper—a grape vineyard.

Bonus Track: Whether you choose to explore St. John's Cemetery or not, **if you don't mind riding in heavy traffic, instead of turning right onto 80th Street (left, if exiting the cemetery), keep straight (left from the cemetery), and follow Metropolitan Avenue east, past St. John's to Cooper Avenue. At Cooper, hang a left and look for house number 89-70.** Due to multiple renovations over the years, it is no longer easily recognizable, but you are standing in front of the house featured in the opening and closing credits as the home of Archie and Edith Bunker in the long-running and wildly popular 1970s TV series *All in the Family.* **From the Bunker house, head back down Cooper Avenue, crossing Metropolitan. Stay on Cooper all the way to Myrtle, just past 71st Street, then cross Myrtle and continue on Cooper, wrapping past the entrance to Cypress Hills Cemetery. (If you chose option #2, turn left from Myrtle onto Cooper and follow Cooper around to Cypress Hills).** Founded in 1848, Cypress Hills Cemetery was the first to be established after adoption of the Rural Cemetery Act. Spread out over two hundred acres (0.81km²) of rolling wooded hills delving into gentle glens revealing an occasional pond, Cypress Hills straddles the boroughs of Brooklyn and Queens. Notable New Yorkers buried here include ragtime, jazz pianist and popular music composer Eubie Blake; first African American and Hall of Fame Major League Baseball player Jackie Robinson; Hollywood screen legend Mae West; and reclusive, hoarding, and cluttering brothers Homer and Langley Collyer—who, sometime after 1919, boarded their windows and withdrew from the world into their 5th Avenue Harlem home, setting booby traps against any who tried to enter. Featured in several movies and works of literature (both fiction and nonfiction), the latest being E. L. Doctorow's recent novel, *Homer and Langley,* rumors hovered around the brothers' filth for decades. But the true extent of their hoarding went undiscovered until their deaths, which occurred just days apart in 1947. Though Langley died first, due to the floor-to-ceiling repository of clutter his body wasn't discovered until three weeks after Homer's. Alerted by an anonymous caller complaining of a putrid smell—possibly a dead body—emanating from the brothers' house, police had to cut through a solid wall of squalor before they could enter the home and find Homer, slumped over his knees, hair matted and tangled in knots, expired on the floor. When the medical examiner placed the time of death at just ten hours earlier, confirming that Homer was not the source their stench, police began the hunt for Langley. After nearly three weeks, and the removal from the premises of 103 tons of refuse, rats were found gorging on Langley's decomposing body, which in the end lay only ten feet from Homer's. He was killed, it appeared, by one of his own booby traps. Paralyzed and reliant on Langley for water and food, Homer died a number of days later from dehydration and starvation.

Follow Cooper around Drumn Circle Park and turn left onto Cypress Hills Street. Stay on Cypress and cross Cooper again on your right, then pick up the bike lane at 78th Avenue. Concentrated on this one-mile strip of winding road are seven cemeteries, all Jewish, and all established between 1850 and 1880, the most notable being Machpelah, where famed magician and escape artist Harry Houdini is buried. Born Ehrich Weiss (in Budapest, Hungary), other than Houdini's grave (who's head has been stolen and vandalized so many times, the New York chapter of American Musicians, which maintains

the shrine, had to remove it altogether), the rest of Machpelah has been largely abandoned. Weeds overrun gravesites, headstones have faded, and decades seem to have passed since the early 1920s office last saw life, human life at least. But for the faint haloed glow flickering over the Houdini grave, Machpelah feels as dead as the bodies interred here. Yet, eerie as it is, standing inside its gates, staring out

at the forgotten overgrown graves, there is a kind of beauty in all this decay, as if you are looking upon a great ancient ruin.

Continue on Cypress Hills Street to Salem Fields Cemetery and turn right onto Jamaica Avenue. Follow Jamaica past the uniform rows of soldiers' graves in National Cemetery to Highland Boulevard. Turn right on Highland and power up the climb, wrapping around the empty Ridgewood Reservoir. Continue wrapping to the right around the Reservoir to Cypress Avenue, turning left on Cypress through Union Field Cemetery (on your right) and Mt. Judah (on your left). Turn right at Cooper Avenue. Ride along Cooper back toward Mt. Neboh and hang left on 62nd Street. Stay on 62nd three blocks to Myrtle Avenue, then turn left onto Myrtle. Follow Myrtle under the railroad trellis and hang an immediate right onto Fresh Pond Road. From Fresh Pond, you have a couple of options for completing the ride.

Option #1: Continue on Fresh Pond to Metropolitan and turn left. Follow Metropolitan to Flushing Avenue, turning right on Flushing to double back to Rust Street. Hang a left at Rust Street, following it all the way back to Greenpoint Avenue and Calvary Cemetery where you started. (Please note: on the way back to Greenpoint Avenue, Rust Street turns first into Laurel Boulevard, then into Review Avenue before it hits Calvary.)

Option #2: Or, if all this death and dying has left you in the mood for a stiff drink, or if you are hungry, instead of returning to Calvary follow Metropolitan into hipsterville Williamsburg, and drop in at any number of watering holes or food dives along Bedford Avenue, including Dumont Burger between South 1st and 2nd, Verve Café at North 5th, or Bike NYC's favorite, Mugs Ale House, at North 10th.

CHAPTER 3

STATEN ISLAND—THE DEAD POOL (ROSSVILLE BOATYARD) (Forty Miles)

THE POOL

Ever wonder where The City's old tugboats go to die? The Dead Pool, also known as the as the Rossville Boatyard.

Ensconced at the edge of the world (from the perspective of New Yorkers) in the shallow waters of Arthur Kill, the tidal strait separating the southernmost tip of the state from its butt-of-bad-jokes neighbor, New Jersey, the boat graveyard, which also entombs the spoiled carcasses of ferries, skiffs, barges, and other retired sea craft, is the marine division of the Donjon Iron and Scrap Metal Processing Facility (a.k.a. the Witte Marine Scrapyard).

Nestled against a backdrop of rusted oil storage tanks and a 225-foot mountain of dirt filling in what was once the world's largest landfill, amid a junk heap of discarded old Conex boxes and auto scraps, the privately owned salvage yard has been disposing of New York's waterway relics since the 1930s. Often considered the city's redheaded stepchild, both by locals

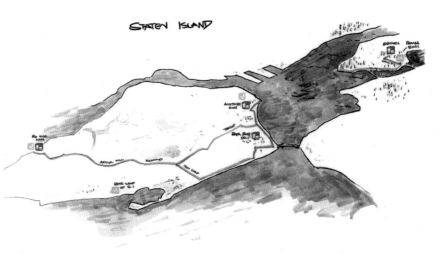

as well as those from the other boroughs, Staten Island is a fitting home for this nautical bone repository; disillusioned by The City's lack of love and services, nearly a century after consolidation, island residents voted to secede from the greater metropolis. Though secession was ultimately quashed by state and city legislatures, the vote illustrated the borough's decades-long frustration with a parental government that, other than collecting its portion of tax revenue, paid the township little attention.

Boats are not so much buried in this graveyard as they are scuttled and left to rot, yet preserved beneath the salty, waterlogged, and sunbaked hulls, as with the people and neighborhoods on this oft-forgotten isle, a textured and storied history lies here. Barcodes to our past scanned from the registers of our present. From the boats themselves, including the *Abram S. Hewitt*—the city's last coal-burning fireboat that aided survivors of the 1904 *PS General Slocum* fire. To Staten Island's residents like Cornelius Vanderbilt—the nineteenth-century steamboat and Staten Island Ferry shipping magnate, to rappers Old Dirty Bastard and Method Man of the Wu Tang Clan, topping a list of numerous others. Among them, generations-long residents Paul and Chace Van Manen, father and son owners of the Bada-Bing American Deli, offering dollar-a-slice pizza across the street from the Bay Street Luncheonette and Soda Fountain, which has served old-fashioned sodas and egg creams since 1939.

The Ride

Fuel up with a cup of coffee and a yummy gluten-free cupcake or slice of banana bread at *Baby Cakes,* New York's kick-a—— vegan bakery at 248 Broome Street between Orchard and Ludlow around the corner from the Tenement Museum on the Lower East Side (LES) of Manhattan. (Note: they only serve drip coffee here; if you are an espresso drinker, **88 Orchard,** less than a block away at Broome and—you guessed it—Orchard, pulls a pretty good one.) If you are short on cash, and/or dietary restrictions, ***sugar Sweet sunshine,*** just north of Delancey Street on Rivington (at Norfolk), might prove the better start point. The owners, Peg and Deb, once worked in Magnolia Bakery on the west side, which was catapulted to fame and fortune after a two-second flash on its storefront in an episode of television's ever-popular *Sex and the City.* Be warned, however! Gender, sexual orientation, views on marriage, and polyamory aside, the pair's chocolate bomb (pudding), or pumpkin trifle might just make you to fall to one knee and present each with a ring.

When satiated, from *Baby Cakes* turn right from Broome onto Ludlow, then pedal south to Grand Avenue and hang a left. (From *sugar Sweet sunshine*, ride west on Rivington, and turn left onto Ludlow. Cross Delancey at the stoplight and continue on toward Grand.) Once on Grand, pedal east past the twenty-story towers of East River Houses (among the first of The City's signature cooperative apartment buildings). **Continue riding through the LES to FDR Drive, then turn right into the designated bike lane, wrapping around Corlears Hook**—the point on the island where the East River hooks north, named after Jacob Van Corlaer, the first Dutch settler on record as owning the land. **Follow the bike lane to Cherry Street and veer right to the entrance to Corlears Hook Park a few hundred feet ahead on your left. Cut through the park**—also named after Jacob Van Corlaer, as well as a play on words as during the mid-1800s, the area was a well-known parade ground for prostitutes servicing the sailors and crewmen who docked at the Hook's port—**to the pedestrian bridge and cross over the highway onto the East River Bikeway, heading south toward the Staten Island Ferry building and Battery Park.**

Recently listed on America's Register of Most Endangered Places, like most of New York (after Peter Minuit's legendary sixty-*guilder* swindle), Manhattan's Lower East Side started its European life as farmland. But by the latter part of the 19th century, as unparalleled numbers of Europeans fled homeland famines, persecutions, and revolutions, the area not only mushroomed into the city's first ghetto, but also festered into one of the nation's worst slums. Prior to the Civil War, racial ghettoes as we know them today did not exist in New York. The poor did reside in slumlike conditions to be sure, more often than not in shantytowns. But in most instances, black, white, and immigrant were all lumped into the same neglected neighborhoods together, within the same dilapidated blocks and falling-down buildings even, regardless of race, religion, or ethnic origin. In enclaves like Seneca Village (razed in the 1850s to make way for Central Park), Irish, Germans, and African Americans worshipped at the same church.

Between 1840 and 1870, millions of new immigrants found their way to New York, with those who stayed totaling two-thirds of the city's population, the majority—over three hundred thousand—squeezing into the mile and a half square parcel known as the Lower East Side. Save a handful of African Americans, precariously sheltered near the waterfront, the Irish arrived first (those who survived the crossing in the coffin ships), in staggering numbers that never seemed to dwindle, and began lining the streets with tenement houses—shoddy apartment buildings, many without toilets or adequate ventilation, four and five stories high harboring in excess of twenty families on lots meant for single occupancy row houses. Sometimes the row houses themselves were converted to tenements, with Ireland's exiled poor spilling into the overcrowded unpaved streets like water through windows in a flood. By the time anybody noticed the tide of the one and a half million Germans that had rolled in beside them, creating the city's first non-English-speaking ghetto, a decade had passed and Manhattanites were calling the area between the Bowery, East 14th, and Division streets, *Kleindeutschland*, or Little Germany. After the 1904 tragedy of the *General Slocum* fire, which consumed the lives of more than one thousand neighborhood women and children, in exceedingly large numbers, the Germans in Little Germany began to vanish, like ghosts, vacating their share of the cramped and crowded real estate for the next swell of non-English-speaking immigrants: Southern Italians, who took up residence on a few streets west of the Bowery and called it Little Italy, and Russian and Eastern European Jews, who for nearly one hundred years made the Lower East Side one of the largest Jewish ghettoes in the world, synonymous with the American Jewish experience at large. In reality, the exodus from *Kleindeutschland* started long before the *General Slocum* caught fire. Wealthier Germans had begun deserting the ghetto two decades earlier, moving uptown to the slightly more hip and spacious Yorkville, along the East River. The *Slocum* fire, and the social and emotional fallout from it, as well as the influx of Italians, Russians, and other Eastern European Jews into the mix, simply hastened the process.

Though still primarily a neighborhood of immigrants (mostly Asian and Hispanic), like Williamsburg and the East Village before it, with its trendy bars, clothing boutiques, restaurants, and coffee shops, today the LES has become a kind of magnet for hipsters. Aside from a few run-down buildings and converted old synagogues, the Tenement Museum and Katz's Bagels (New York's oldest kosher-style deli, dating back to 1888), little of The City's first ghetto remains.

Continue riding south along the bikeway toward the Manhattan Bridge, past the Fiorello LaGuardia housing projects—owned and operated since 1957 by the New York City Housing Authority (NYCHA), the first such public housing corporation in the country. **Ride under the overpass of the fourth oldest bridge in The City** (behind the Brooklyn, Williamsburg, and Queensboro spans, completed in 1909, on a design by Leon Moisseiff), the last of the three suspension bridges joining the boroughs of Brooklyn and Manhattan.

Gaze out over the channel at the ebb and flow of the murky East River and listen. Past the horns honking and the sirens whaling, the subway trains rattling overhead on the bridge, helicopters circling the skyline. Over the ever-present cacophony of noise that drives this town, the engine that keeps it moving forward. Can you hear them? The ghosts of the bodies?

Formed some eleven thousand years ago at the end of the last ice age, New York City's other river, which is really not a river at all, but a tidal strait, much like the Arthur Kill, has likely had more dead bodies fished from its surface than almost any other river in the world, except perhaps, the Ganges. Can you see them? From disaster casualties like those aboard the *General Slocum* to the bridge jumpers, mob hits, and targets of crooked cops, to those who just walked out of their apartments one day and were never heard from again until the weather began to thaw and their corpses were found floating on the surface of the river, facedown, half-decomposed and bloated, the victims of mishap and foul play as much as suicide and catastrophe. Like R. Lester Cornell, who in 1905 said goodnight to his friends at the corner of 31st and Broadway, then walked into the dark and disappeared, or Svetlana Aronov, who vanished from the Upper East Side during an afternoon walk with the family dog. Columbia computer engineering student Richard Ng never returned after leaving cam-

pus one night a week before graduation. Even tourists have gotten into the act; Jeanette Stiteler, visiting from Arizona, leapt to her death from the stern of a Circle Line boat in the middle of a tour around the island, while the most famous body to date would have to be Spalding Gray—the renowned writer and actor, best known for his one-man show turned documentary, *Swimming to Cambodia,* among numerous other credits, who departed his flat in Tribeca in January 2004, then turned up in the river in March.

Across the way on the eastern bank, the Brooklyn waterfront—from the rocky beach at Brooklyn Bridge and Empire-Fulton Ferry State Park—offers unparalleled views of the bridges and the Manhattan skyline, especially on a warm summer night, lapping at a cone from the **Brooklyn Ice Cream Factory,** just down the shore to the south in a restored 1920s fireboat house at the Fulton Ferry Landing—the historic harbor from which under cover of storm and fog, in commandeered fishing boats, Revolutionary War general George Washington evacuated his beleaguered and painfully outnumbered Continental Army troops from the disastrous Battle of Brooklyn. The deft and clandestine move allowed Washington and his troops to live to fight another day as the saying goes; having sustained heavy losses and casualties (nearly three thousand American soldiers were killed or taken prisoner in just a few hours of fighting, compared with just a few hundred for the British), had the cloaked withdrawal failed, the war for independence may have ended in Brooklyn Heights, rather than Yorktown, with a very different outcome.

Continue riding on the bikeway past Chinatown toward the Brooklyn Bridge, the City's first, completed in 1883, on a design by wire rope pioneer John Augustus Roebling. Unfortunately, the German-born engineer never lived to see his iconic span finished. In fact, he never saw it begin. While surveying the future site of his dream project, his most ambitious yet as the longest suspension bridge in the world (at time of completion), a docking ferry boat rocked the pier on which Roebling was standing, crushing one of his feet against a pylon. Three weeks later, having refused further treatment after his toes were amputated, he died from tetanus.

Roebling's dream was kept alive by his eldest son, Washington, an engineer in his own right, who had signed on as his father's assistant. But just three years into Washington's reign as chief, the younger Roebling was stricken with a condition called the bends, also known as caisson disease, or decompression sickness. In order to anchor the stone towers of one of the world's landmark bridges, three-thousand-ton wooden boxes, with the bottoms cut out, called caissons, were sunk to the bed of the river, then pumped with compressed air to force out the water. From inside these pressure chambers as they were, accessed through a tube in the top called a "Man Shaft," disoriented workers manned hydraulic jacks, shovels, wheelbarrows, and other excavation tools to hollow out the sediment in search of the bedrock deep beneath the river. At the end of a day's shift, upon emerging from the caissons to the surface, the rapid return to normal air pressure caused many of the workers to fall ill. Convinced that a catastrophic accident would result if he did not personally oversee the work, Roebling spent as much if not more time in the chambers than the men he supervised. Although a handful of caisson workers died from the disease, most—like Washington—suffered paralysis. Finally, after one too many descents into the caissons, the younger Roebling collapsed and had to be removed from the site, forced to observe the remainder of construction through a telescope set up in the bedroom window of his town house.

The unsung hero in this epic saga then, responsible at least for the turning of her husband's and father-in-law's dreams into reality (if not for the existence of the bridge itself), was Washington's wife, Emily, Emily Warren Roebling. Not only did Emily convince the powers that be to keep her husband on as chief engineer, from Washington, on the fly she learned the basic principles of structural engineering in order to better communicate problems and solutions between the engineer and the work site, which she ferried back and forth on a daily basis. Eleven years later, on May 24, 1883, 1,800 vehicles and 150,000 pedestrians crossed the long-anticipated East River Bridge, the first to connect the island of Manhattan to Brooklyn. For overseeing its completion, Emily Warren Roebling could arguably be called the world's first female engineer.

Chinatown

After the gold rush, in spite of the Chinese Exclusion Act, which from 1882 to 1943 barred Chinese nationals already in the country from naturalizing as citizens, and those living without from entering altogether, with a specific prohibition levied against women and children. Chinese immigration during the nineteenth and early twentieth centuries, albeit extremely gender lopsided, trickled into the United States without interruption. Those who found their way to New York, legally or otherwise, settled in the few square blocks of the LES south of Houston Street, east of Broadway, north of Chambers and Frankfort Streets, and east of Clinton, Ridge, and Essex Streets.

Like most ethnic arrivals before and since, they faced a rash of discrimination based on difference, and the fear that by their willingness to work on the cheap in unsafe conditions the immigrants were stealing jobs from the white working poor. As a result, the growing number of Chinese in New York not only kept to themselves, but in most regards, established a thriving, self-sufficient community. An off-the-grid system of associations and commerce collected taxes, provided jobs, housing, financial support, recreation (often in the form of opium dens and prostitution), as well as insurance—protection from the always-smoldering systemic and political racism that too often erupted in violence. The neighborhood became so well insulated from the rest of The City, that even today, for goods and services, the average Chinatown resident seldom needs travel outside its ever-increasing boundaries. Unlike other immigrant groups, who as fortunes grew left the ghetto behind to blend into the so-called melting pot, after the Exclusion Act was lifted along with other immigration restrictions in 1968, the neighborhood ballooned into the largest concentration of Chinese in the Western world.

Though still an ethnic enclave, today Chinatown is showing the signs of a neighborhood in flux. Hipsters—read young, fresh out of art school, and looking for a party—in what may indicate the first wave of gentrification into the one City neighborhood considered immune, have begun sloshing over across Delancey from the slightly more pricey LES to take up residence in the land of $2 dumplings, noodles, and sesame-seed pancakes. A sunny-day stroll—or ride in this case—down Mott Street, Grand, or Hester, on what used to seem a far-flung journey through a strange and exotic land where the odor of raw fish seemed to permeate even the residents, and the temperature often felt ten degrees hotter than anywhere else in The City, now reveals new disparate clips of "Dude!" and other American phrases regularly fractured between the Mandarin and Cantonese streaming from the windows of the tenement-style apartment buildings here.

A few of Bike NYC's neighborhood favorites? **Vanessa's Dumpling House** at 118 Eldridge between Grand and Broome, around the corner from the Bike Polo courts at Sarah Roosevelt Park. Or, just down the street, also on Eldridge between Hester and Canal, and just as good *sans* the wait and the hype and cheaper—if you can believe it—**Prosperity Dumpling** proves a nice alternative. For a true Chinatown nightlife experience, we recommend **Winnie's**, at 104 Bayard Street between Baxter and Mulberry, possibly the best—or worst depending on who you ask—karaoke bar in the city. It's tiny, tacky, smelly, in desperate need of repairs, complete with Chinese locals holed up at the bar on one side, and next-wave hipsters in the booths on the other. Run by a former Peking opera star who offers a dated pre-1995 play list of a thousand songs at a dollar per song (with a two drink minimum), including a fair selection of Mandarin pop tunes, like most things New York, you will either love this place, or hate it. (**Bike NYC special note:** if you plan to sample the Hawaiian punch here, you might consider taking the train home.)

After passing Chinatown, you have a couple of options for sweeping around the financial district past Wall Street—which used to be a wall, raised by the Dutch to keep out the natives—before heading on to the Staten Island Ferry Building. Depending on your obstacle course preferences—bipeds or motorcars—you can either remain on the bikeway, which weaves around to the left into a tangled web of pedestrian/bicycle shared detours, utilizing sidewalks and makeshift replacement corridors courtesy of DOT construction (at the time of this writing), or bunny hop onto South Street and twine instead through the lanes of traffic, making sure to stay to the right to keep from entering the South Street Viaduct (unless, of course, you're looking to pull a Brendan McMullen). *(Bike NYC should note here that just like the tunnels it is illegal to ride your bike through the viaduct and we do not recommend doing so.)*

At Broad Street, hand-signal into the left-turn lane and hop up onto the sidewalk—after making the turn—to the right of the Battery Maritime Building (where the Governors Island Ferry departs from), and cruise around to the front of the Staten Island Ferry terminal (the sloped glass building next door). Enter the terminal—walking, of course—and follow the prompts and instructions for bicycles. *(Please note: you will be searched here, as well as on the way back, and sniffed by a guard dog, as will your bike.)*

If you wish to remain on the path, follow the detours

until you reach the Maritime Building, then duplicate the directions in the South Street option.

In the 1700s, before the Richmond Turnpike Company ran the first steam-powered ferry service between Richmond County (Staten Island) and Manhattan, passengers were trafficked back and forth across the upper New York Bay by sailboat. In 1838, Cornelius Vanderbilt purchased a controlling share in the RTC and created a fleet of orange boats known as the Staten Island Ferry, whose frothy white wakes can be seen for miles crisscrossing the harbor. Outfitted with racks to secure their bike, cyclists are relegated to the lower cabin. Bathrooms are located in the upper, as is the snack bar, which also serves beer. The crossing takes about twenty-five minutes and makes up 5.2 miles of the entire ride.

Step out onto the deck as you steam past the 305-foot Statue of Liberty (a quarter of the height of the Empire State Building, foundation to torch), the best view going of the Lady these days next to Ellis Island and the Circle Line cruise. Perhaps better as the ferry service is free. Look out over the bay and imagine it the way Henry Hudson's crew first saw it when they passed through the Narrows. Or the Huguenots, the first 150 colonists. A warm autumn day, the water a deep unspoiled blue. Oak, chestnut, maple, and hickory trees—where skyscrapers now stand—lining the shores. Meadows, swamps, salt marshes, and ponds—in place of squares—that once fed beaver, deer, turkeys, and bear. Footpaths worn over millenia winding through the forests in place of traffic-snarled streets and highways.

Exit the Ferry at St. George Terminal, then ride up the viaduct to Richmond Terrace, which turns into Bay Street, and turn left. Named after George Law, a land baron who gave up the property for the terminal in exchange for the sainthood reflected in the neighborhood's moniker, as the borough's seat of government, St. George is the most densely populated neighborhood on the island. If the SIF snack bar didn't suit you, or you require a bit more coffee to recharge from the insulin spike suffered after the fuel-up at sugar Sweet sunshine, or you are struck with a sudden urge to forgo the bike and sit in a garden and read a book for a while, listen to a record or two or bust out an acoustic number on a borrowed guitar, stop in at **Every Thing Goes Books Café and Neighborhood Stage,** just past Victory on the west side of Bay Street. The name, in its matter-of-fact expression of duality, is a possible theme for the island as well. Staten Island is a place still trying to make sense of itself after 350 years.

Continue on Bay Street to Hannah and make a left at the Mobile station. Follow Hannah over the SIR (Staten Island Railway), then drop down to the right onto Murray Hulbert Avenue, which turns into Front Street, which in turn becomes Edgewater Drive. Pedal along the water past Millers Launch, through the island's industrial northeast shore, the Verrazano Bridge suspended ahead on the horizon, Brooklyn's Belt Parkway on the other side of the Narrows, wrapping around Gravesend Bay into Coney Island in the distance. Follow Edgewater until it dead-ends at Fort Wadsworth.

Past the New York State School of Bartending (licensed and accredited by the New York State Department of Education), the Queen Anne Car Wash and Top Tomato Super Store, the Saturn dealership, Bay Street Luncheonette and Soda Fountain, and the Van Manen's Bada Bing American Deli. Pedal past the homes of the island's wealthiest and notorious residents, including Paul Castellano, the Gambino crime family boss rubbed out by "Dapper Don" John Gotti. His $3.5 million home was built to mimic 1600 Pennsylvania Avenue, in Washington DC.

Ride past the guard shack and enter Fort Wadsworth, the control

center for the City's arm of the Nike missile defense system during the years of the Cold War. Initially fortified by the British at the start of the war for independence, prior to decommission in 1994, the battery installations here served as the guardians of the maritime gateway to the City for more than two hundred years. **Spin under the Verrazano-Narrows Bridge,** the last major public works project pushed through by Robert Moses, named after Giovanni da Verrazzano, the first European explorer to sail into the New York Harbor. **Turn right onto Battery Road, which turns into McClean Avenue. Ride two blocks past Lilly Pond Avenue then swing a left at Sands Lane across Father Capodanno Boulevard. Cut through the parking lot to the right of the dolphin fountain and jump onto the FDR Boardwalk,** at two and a half miles, the fourth longest boardwalk in the world. Also home to SI's free summer concerts. **Follow the boardwalk all the way to the end past the abandoned hangars at Miller Field,** the first East Coast air defense station and the last of The City's grass-runway airports. **Wrap to the right around the base through the parking lot (looks more like an old gravel road to nowhere) and turn right from the exit onto New Dorp Lane. Continue along New Dorp to Richmond Road and turn left. (New Dorp can get bogged down with congestion as you approach Hylan Boulevard so remain extra alert here.)**

Roll through the turns around Richmond Road to Arthur Kill Road and enter Historic Richmond Town, an outdoor living museum, complete with reenactments, dedicated to preserving the neighborhood's colonial past as the seat of county government and the island's center of commerce preconsolidation. After the borough joined with Greater New York, the parent government relocated management of the island's affairs to St. George, which was closer to Manhattan. Trade and business followed, and Richmondtown was abandoned. The Historic Richmond Town project began with the salvage and restoration of the mid-nineteenth-century county clerk's and surrogate's office in 1932. Since then, fifteen of the museum's twenty-seven buildings have been given new life, including the oldest known schoolhouse in the country, dating back to 1695, and several others rescued from demolition and moved here from other areas of the island.

Turn left onto Arthur Kill Road and wrap around past the Voorlezer's House—the little red seventeenth-century schoolhouse—and

the William T. Davis Wildlife Refuge, under the West Shore Expressway on your way to Rossville, the 225-foot mound of the former Fresh
Kills Landfill stalking you to the west as you ride. (This road generally
caries a high volume of traffic moving at a pretty good clip. Although
the fairly wide shoulder leaves plenty of room for riding—even with
cars parked on the side of the road—keep your head up here.)

As you approach the Lava Lounge, the former Waterloo Café, slow
up and look to your right. Built into the short retaining wall on the side
of the road, you will find a set of stairs leading to one of the island's—if
not one of the City's—oldest and smallest cemeteries.

In Blazing Star Burial Ground, scratched into the faces of the tombstones still legible, are the names of some of the island's—as well as New
York's—first families. The remains in this once-abandoned graveyard,
salvaged and maintained by the Friends of Abandoned Cemeteries, span
nearly one hundred years and date to the mid-seventeenth century. They
are the same names emblazoned on street signs around here, the City's
last working farm, located of course in Historic Richmond Town. Some
were believed Huguenots, tracing their lineage back to the first settlers of
the City.

Blazing Star—after the Blazing Star Tavern—was the original name
for the town of Rossville, until it was changed in the 1830s to honor Col.
William E. Ross, the Revolutionary War hero who built a replica of England's Windsor Castle as his home on the edge of a cliff overlooking the
Blazing Star Ferry landing. The landing is now home to the Donjon Iron
and Scrap Metal Processing Facility.

Cross to the break in the tree cover on the other side of the cemetery

to see the boats, as well as traces
of the abandoned landing pier. If
you would like to move closer, the
best path to the Pool lies beyond a
BE WARE OF DOG sign, suspended
by chain across the driveway of
the pre–Civil War frame house a

few hundred feet to the south at the junction of Arthur Kill Road and Rossville Avenue. The dog sign is no bluff, so **make sure to knock on the door and ask permission first** before traipsing off through private property. In general, the owners don't mind as long as you ask.

If you need to refuel, or use the bathroom before heading back, or wish to sample a bit of live local color after communing with the dead, stop in at **Big Nose Kate's Saloon (2484 Arthur Kill Road),** Rossville's Western-themed bar and restaurant, complete with rusted-through horseshoes grafted into the concrete porch steps like kill notches on gun barrels, just around the bend to the south past St. Luke's Avenue.

Otherwise, **pedal back the way you came, along Arthur Kill**

Road back through Historic Richmond Town to Richmond Road. Follow Richmond Road, circling around the mansions hovering on Todt Hill, until it turns into Targee Street. From Targee turn right onto Vanderbilt Avenue and weave through the middle-class neighborhood of Stapleton, former site of the Vanderbilt family farm, as well as the present location of Park Hill Apartments and Stapleton Houses, the federal- and state-subsidized housing projects where Ghostface Killah, Method Man, and other members of nineties hip-hop phenoms the Wu-Tang Clan cut their chops. The *One Flew Over the Cuckoo's Nest*-looking building, rising up across the street from Park Hill as you reach Bay Street, is Bayley Seaton Hospital. Opened in 1831 as the Seaman's Retreat for retired sailors, the hospital now serves as SI's psychiatric and social services outpatient facility.

From Vanderbilt, turn left onto Bay Street an return to St. George and the Ferry.

On The Wheel

NAME: SULYN SILBAR
AGE: 43

BIKE: OLD SCHOOL TREK 400

CHAPTER 4

MANHATTAN/QUEENS—ART CRAWL (Ten Miles)

The Art

The department of tourism counts more than eighty-five museums in New York City. Eighty-five official repositories dedicated to the preservation of dreams, feats, endeavors, leaps of faith, and genius, all of it evidence of our time here. From the big guns, the renowned halls of meteorites, habitat dioramas and fossils in the Museum of Natural History, the Van Goghs, Cèzannes, and Picassos in the MoMa (Museum of Modern Art), to the lesser known cabinets of the American Numismatic Society, or the decommissioned tunnels of The City's Transit Museum. They are our hieroglyphs and cave drawings, time capsules for the future we've never buried, but displayed and illuminated for all to see and contribute to, generation after generation, in the telling and retelling of our collective story. Our roots, ever reminding us of who we are, where we come from, and where we are going. In this tradition, on a two-borough ride through Upper Manhattan and Northwest Queens, Bike NYC invites you

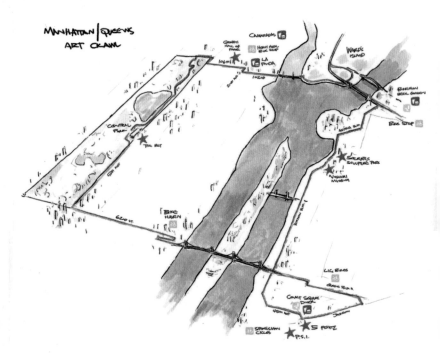

to explore some of the art, voices, and neighborhoods less traveled in the City's narrative.

The Graffiti Hall of fame

LOCATION: PUBLIC JUNIOR HIGH SCHOOL 13, EAST 106TH STREET AND PARK AVENUE, MANHATTAN

Locked inside a chain-link fence in *El Barrio* Spanish Harlem, the walls enclosing the sunken playground of the Jackie Robinson Education Complex—Public Junior High School 13—provided the first legal canvas for graffiti writers in the City. Founded in 1980 by East Harlem community activist Ray Rodriguez, space on the wall is offered only to those writers who have had a major impact on hip-hop and graffiti culture in one of the four major disciplines: rhyming, writing, Dj'ing, and break dancing. Famous OG writers who've tattooed these walls, graff artists that have been around since the beginning, include Cope2 (alias Fernando Carlo)—the South Bronx native who grabbed mainstream attention with his 2005 *Time* magazine billboard ad on the side of a building in Soho; Futura 2000 (Leonard Hilton McGurr)—an old-school bike messenger, recently commissioned to paint a limited edition track bike designed and produced by master frame builder Ernesto Colnago; and the TATS Cru—also from the Bronx. The TATS Cru was founded by Bio (Wilfredo Feliciano), Nicer (Hector Nazario), and BG183 (Sotero Ortiz), pioneer writers noted for their continuing efforts to raise the public view of graffiti from vandalism to art. These days, not only is the crew one of the most sought-after mural and "graff art" companies in commercial advertising, but its members have become lecturers giving presentations on the art and history of graffiti to universities as well as innumerable local community groups, organizations, and public schools.

In a subtle bit of irony, in the summer of 2009 the Hall of Fame's walls were "vandalized," tagged over by practitioners of the very same art form the founders sought to legitimize. It is believed it was done in protest against the "permit only" selective-access policy to the hall's hallowed canvas.

Socrates Sculpture Garden (Park)

LOCATION: 31-34 VERNON BLVD (BTWN 31ST AND BROADWAY), LONG ISLAND CITY, QUEENS

Tucked away on a 4.5-acre scratch of landfill along the riverfront in Long Island City, with the Manhattan skyline in the background, Socrates Sculpture Park embodies the drive, inspiration, creativity, and resilience that feeds this town. It represents what calls so many of us to come and make our mark here and add our voices to the fray. A former illegal dumping ground, the sculpture garden is the brainchild of celebrated abstract expressionist sculptor Mark Suvero. In the same spirit that compelled New Yorkers to weep and volunteer their skills, their hands and hearts in the aftermath of Ground Zero, the same spirit of mobilization and outrage—fueled by nineteenth-century photographer Jacob Riis' haunting portraits of tenement life in *How the Other Half Lives*—led to passage of the New York State Tenement House Act. In response to the act, a collaboration of artists, neighborhood residents, friends, family, volunteers, politicians, benefactors, and untold others joined together to reclaim a piece of urban blight and revive it into a large-scale outdoor museum, an emerging artist-in-residence studio and a lush green much-needed neighborhood park, home to some of the coolest jungle gyms in the world.

Conceived in 1985, a nearly-five-year undertaking, a couple of grants and a lot of love and nurturing later, the Socrates Sculpture Garden is like no

other public exhibition space or park in the City. Unlike other galleries and museums, kids as well as adults are not only encouraged to touch here, but to climb and hang and otherwise interact with the art and the artists who created it. In addition to a great art show, the garden offers fitness classes, sculpture workshops for kids, sustainable urban survival skills workshops for adults, a

Makers Market, along with a popular summer outdoor cinema (Wednesday nights at 7:00 PM, July and August), concerts, discussions, and much, much more. Although some events require advance registration, all programs are free and open to the public.

5 Pointz

LOCATION: 46-23 CRANE STREET (OFF JACKSON AVENUE AND 46TH STREET), LONG ISLAND CITY, QUEENS (ACROSS THE STREET FROM PS1)

Dubbed by its curator the "Institute of Higher Burnin,'" for the last fifteen years, the outside walls of a two-hundred-thousand-square-foot factory building-turned-illegal-artist's-lofts, known as the 5 Pointz Aerosol Art Center, Inc., have played host to what is deemed the mecca of graffiti writers and artists around the world. Named for the five boroughs of Greater New York City, 5 Pointz was an aerosol oasis in the midst of a landscape that Mayor Koch parched of color during his 1980s graffiti crackdown. The institute was founded in 1994 by Pat DeLillo, a former neighborhood plumber who, until he had a change of heart and gained an appreciation for some of the artists' talents, ran an antigraffiti gang called the graffiti terminators. Armed with cans of paint and rollers, the terminators fanned through the streets and alleyways covering up what DeLillo then considered a scourge upon the neighborhood. In time, however, through DeLillo's close interaction with the tags, he grew to view them as art. The former plumber reached the revelation that just as everyone who picks up a brush and sits in front of an easel does *not* produce a Rembrandt, not every bubble tag spray-painted across a wall or billboard is equal either. A hierarchy exists, based largely on talent, and just like the art forms society already applauds there are amateurs, and pros as well as hacks and copycats. And, individual taste aside, a piece's brilliance is not determined by where it hangs or however temporary the medium; a piece of graffiti can be as evocative as the works exhibited in the Modern Mueusm of Art's PS1 Contemporary Art Center.

Upon realizing that he actually liked a lot of the work he was erasing, DeLillo decided to start helping artists instead of fighting them by securing "legal" walls for them to paint without threat or fear of arrest. And while much of the lure for illegal writing involves the danger, thrill, and fame of throwing up a tag in a forbidden zone and getting away with it, the idea of having stress-free unlimited time to create larger more intricate "pieces" (often taking days to complete), as well as the promise of leaving them on display for longer periods of time, in most cases proved the bigger carrot. After talking one of his clients into letting the artists use the outside walls of his factory building as their canvas, what DeLillo called the Phun Factory became an instant success, hosting nearly two hundred graffiti writers per year (until it closed six years later due to a dispute between DeLillo and the factory building owner).

In 2001, under new curatorship, Johnathan Cohen, known in the graff world by his famous tag Meres One, reopened the Phun Factory as 5 Pointz. Unlike the Hall of Fame, and nearly fifteen times the size, all artists regardless of skill level are permitted to paint here. All they have to do is ask. None of the artists are paid, and time and space on the walls are provided for free. Depth of artistry and length of effort determine how long a piece stays up. The better ones can remain for years.

For viewing, 5 Pointz is open 24/7. Writers must consult with Meres for an appointment time.

Bonus Tracks

The Noguchi Museum

LOCATION: 32-37 VERNON BOULEVARD, LONG ISLAND CITY, QUEENS

Isamu Noguchi was a major Japanese American sculptor, artist, landscape architect, furniture and set designer. The love child of Japanese poet Yone Noguchi and New York-born American writer and editor Leonie Gilmour, the sculptor passed his formative years traveling back and forth with his mother between the United Sates and Japan and all points in between. In addition to his sculptures, during a career that lasted some sixty years Noguchi crafted numerous stage sets for celebrated choreographer Martha Graham, and designed one of the first electronic baby monitors, the Radio Nurse, commissioned, manufactured, and sold by the Zenith corporation in 1937. Some of his large-scale public works can still be seen across the globe in France, Japan, and Israel as well as throughout the United States.

The Noguchi Museum was opened in 1985 by the artist himself in a converted factory building; the museum represents the largest collection of the artist's works under a single roof with thirteen galleries and a basalt and granite sculpture garden.

PS1 Contemporary Art Center
LOCATION: 22-25 JACKSON AVENUE, LONG ISLAND CITY, QUEENS

The PS1 Contemporary Art Center is the branch of the Modern Museum of Art committed to the exhibition of artworks produced since World War II. Opened in 1976 by former director Alanna Heiss, co-founder of the Institute for Art and Urban Resources along with critic and architecture preservationist the late Brendan Gill, PS1 is the culmination of the institute's vision and goal of transforming the city's abandoned buildings into cutting-edge alternative exhibition spaces for site-specific art. Named after the first public school in Long Island City, which occupied the building until it closed at the dawn of the civil rights movement, the center is considered one of the oldest and most substantial art institutions in the country. Notable artists on permanent display here include op art painter and illustrator Richard Artschwager, animator William Kentridge, and world-renowned video artist Pipilotti Rist.

The Ride

Begin on East Drive in Manhattan's famed Central Park, between East 81st and 82nd streets behind the Metropolitan Museum of Art across from Cleopatra's Needle—the park's 3,500-year-old Egyptian Obelisk.

The oldest man-made object in the park, there are differing accounts as to how we came to possess such an ancient artifact, some of them reconciled in history books, confirmed by conjecture and rumor. Why it is nicknamed Cleopatra's Needle remains a bit of a puzzle though, as neither the park monument nor its twin on the bank of the Thames River in London, or a third in Paris that also bears the name, has anything to do with the fabled monarch other than the fact that all hail from Egypt. Each predates the lady Cleo's arrival on this planet by nearly 1,500 years, the twins in London and New York, on the orders of Tuthmosis III (the sixth pharaoh of the same dynasty that produced King Tut), sometime between 1479 and 1425 BC at the entrance to one of his many temples.

One of the printed narratives regarding procurement of the City's needle is that some 3,500 years after its creation in 1877, the khedive of Egypt offered the *hieroglyphed* pillar to us as a gift for remaining neutral when European interests attempted to gain political control over the

Egyptian government. Another suggests that the khedive gave us the tattooed column as a gesture of goodwill in an effort to increase trade between our two nations. The rumored version? We stole it. The notion that we could have stolen the obelisk—difficult as it is to believe, given that the solid granite pillar stands seventy-one feet tall and tips the scales at 244 tons—is not without precedent. After all, we have faced such accusations before. Remember George Gray Barnard and the Cloisters?

Perhaps the most impressive fact about Cleopatra's Needle, stolen or otherwise, was the two-year odyssey undertaken to bring it here. Coaxed along by a combination of block and tackle, trestle, rollers, and a steam engine, the two-mile crosstown journey from the Hudson River along West 96th Street to its current location in the park took almost four months. It has sustained some damage over the years: repeated exposure to inclement weather and pollution has eroded most of the hieroglyphs, and the four crab claws at the base are replicas. The originals were cast in bronze sometime around 12 BC by the Romans—to replace the broken-off corners—after Augustus Caesar relocated the obelisk from its birthplace in Heliopolis to the capital of Alexandria. While in Alexandria, the story goes, two of the original crabs were stolen. The other two are on permanent display in the building behind you, the Metropolitan Museum of Art (the Met), which begins the section of Fifth Avenue known as "Museum Mile."

From the Met, at fourteen acres in size, one of the largest art museums in the world, with over two million square feet of floor space displaying an even greater number of artworks, **ride north, shadowing Fifth Avenue, along East Drive through the park toward Harlem.**

The result of a design competition held in 1857, Central Park is one of the most visited public man-made landscapes in the world, the four-by-fifty-one-block rectangle in the middle of Manhattan, was the first such enterprise conceived and realized by Frederick Law Olmsted and Calvert Vaux (that's *Voks,* not *Vo* as it is often mispronounced). At 843 acres (imagine the same number of football fields laid side to side and end to end), tour guides are fond of revealing that the only thing natural included in the pair's winning "Greensward" plan are the big rock outcroppings that once studded the entire island, the Manhattan schist, dotted throughout the rectangle. Everything else including the gentle rolling hills you've been pedaling has been cleared, shaped, blasted with gunpowder, excavated, tunneled, planted, and drained into submission according to duo's grand vision. While Olmsted, New York's parks superintendent at the time, is given most of the credit for artistry and design, it was Vaux who was the experienced architect in both structure and landscape. Without his creative contributions to function and form, the park would be minus a number of the features for which it is so often praised.

Employing over twenty thousand workers, who along with planting over 270,000 trees and shrubs, created paths, roads, and bridges winding around meadows, forests, ponds, and lakes, Central Park was constructed in just a little over a year, opening in the winter of 1859 just in time for ice skating season on its new ponds. A victim of the same damage and neglect that befell the rest of the City's parks during the 1970s and '80s, Central Park was completely restored to its original luster. Today the park maintains more than twenty-six thousand trees (including one of the largest surviving groves of American elm trees in the country, lining the Mall to Bethesda Terrace), nine thousand lawns, nearly four dozen ballfields and playgrounds, fifty-five sculptures, thirty-six bridges, open-air concert and theater stages, a band shell, a reservoir, and a zoo.

Look to your right as you spin along Museum Mile, passing in order, the Goethe-Institut, one of five U.S. cultural institutions sponsored by the Federal Republic of Germany, **the Neue Gallerie New York,** a museum dedicated to the preservation of early-twentieth-century German and Austrian art and design, followed by **the Solomon R. Guggenheim Museum,** designed by Frank Lloyd Wright, aside from a house on Lighthouse Hill in Staten Island, the only Frank Lloyd Wright structure in the City as well as the last the famous architect would render (Lloyd Wright died six months before the museum opened). Although somewhat controversial the year it was completed in 1959, critics believing that the inventive composition of the building overshadowed the art it was constructed to exhibit, today the Guggenheim is recognized as one of the premier modern and contemporary art museums in the world, with Frank Lloyd Wright's spiraling swan song the centerpiece of its collection. **From the Guggenheim, continue on along East Drive and Museum Mile past Cooper-Hewitt, the Jewish and City Museums, and** *El Museo del Barrio.*

On the downhill around the pool, stay to your right and exit the park, following the sign directing you toward Lenox Avenue. Turn right at the stoplight onto West 110th Street and follow 110th around

Frawley Circle and exit onto 5th Avenue. Stay on 5th Avenue to East 106th Street and hang a left.

Welcome to Spanish Harlem! Of roughly four million Puerto Ricans currently residing in the United States, nearly a quarter of them, the largest assemblage outside Puerto Rico, live in New York City, with the majority concentrated in the area snuggled up against the Harlem and East rivers between East 96th Street and 5th Avenue, locally christened *El Barrio.*

From the 1880s through the 1950s, much of *El Barrio* was originally known as Italian Harlem, after Sicilian and other Southern Italian immigrants turned the neighborhood into upper Manhattan's Little Italy. The first wave of Puerto Ricans began arriving after World War I, taking up residence just off Central Park near Lexington Avenue and East 110th Street. As bridges began straddling the East River like sparkling bejeweled ladder rungs, the Brooklyn Bridge first, followed by the Williamsburg, Queensboro, Manhattan, and Robert F. Kennedy (Triboro), more and more Puerto Ricans made their way to a better life on the mainland, filling in the space left by Italian immigrants, who traveled across the river for more spacious housing. By the time the race riots hit in the 1960s, and the rent strikes, (organized in Central and Spanish Harlem by the Black Panther and Young Lords parties), the Puerto Rican presence had grown so large that it ate up the last of the Italian outposts in Harlem.

Famous residents who have called the barrio home include Tito Puente, the mambo and jazz "king of Latin music"; rock-and-roll legend and bad girl Ronnie Spector; and Piri Thomas, author of the 1967 best seller *Down These Mean Streets.*

Today, like its Central Harlem cousin to the west, demographically, *El Barrio* is changing. While still predominantly Puerto Rican, other Hispanics, including Mexicans and Dominicans, as well as Middle Eastern and other immigrants, have begun moving into the area .

From the Graffiti Hall of Fame (East 106th Street and Park Avenue), continue on 106th under the Park Avenue Viaduct to 2nd Avenue and turn right. Follow 2nd Avenue to East 102nd Street. At 2nd hang

a left toward the river. If you are in need of bike shop or are hungry and wish to sample some of the neighborhood fare, **Heavy Metal Bike Shop** is located at **2016 3rd Avenue between East 110th and 111th (closer to 111th),** and home-style Puerto Rican cooking is available at **La Fonda Boriqua at 169 East 106th between Lexington and 3rd avenues. Or, if you don't mind veering off route a bit, drop in at Camaradas, a local dive bar and restaurant with $15 pitchers of sangria and decent light food choices like chicken wraps, on 1st Avenue between 115th and 116th streets.**

If you elect not to stop, after crossing 1st Avenue midway through the block on the left, at the driveway leading to the East River housing project garbage dumpsters, ride up onto the sidewalk and veer around the corner on the walled-in walkway to the left along the FDR to the ramp of the Wards Island pedestrian and bicycle bridge. Ride up the ramp, the ramp follows the walkway across the FDR and the East River. Stop for a minute and peer back over the declarations of love and other bridge-wall tags through the prison-green chain-link fence and absorb the less celebrated views of the City. The mouth of the Harlem River to the north winds between upper Manhattan and the Bronx. Midtown and Mill Rock Island to the south, floating singular and alone in the middle of the East River, marking the entrance to the ominous Hell Gate strait whose treacherous rock outcroppings once caused the sinking of hun-

dreds of vessels trying to navigate its currents on the way to Long Island Sound, including the HMS *Hussar,* an English Revolutionary War frigate, rumored to be carrying nearly $5 million dollars in gold.

Mill Rock Island, named after a mill built upon it in 1701, has morphed through a number of incarnations before evolving into its current form: from the aforementioned mill, to an illegal squatter farm, to another unused fort constructed to defend the New York Harbor against the British during the War of 1812. Originally a link in a chain of three islands, Great Mill Rock, Little Mill Rock, and Flood Rock, in 1885 the islands were detonated into one when the City of New York used nearly 150 tons of dynamite and other explosives to obliterate Flood Rock (the most hazardous of the three). This set off the largest orchestrated explosion in history until the first atomic bomb test at the White Sands Proving Ground in southern New Mexico. The shockwaves from the New York blast were felt as far away as Princeton, New Jersey, with the leftover bits and pieces of the former Flood Rock not utterly incinerated used as landfill to join Great Mill and Little Mill Rocks into the solitary Mill Rock. Another Robert Moses Public Works creation, with topsoil added, trees and shrubs planted, and large rocks and boulders brought in to fortify the shore against erosion, the present-day four-acre island plays host to Mill Rock Park, a nesting preserve for egrets and other harbor herons, and at the time of this writing closed to the public.

Pedal over the footbridge, chasing your shadow over the climb and descent like a breakaway ghost rider, and drop down onto Wards Island. (*Note: A lift bridge, November through March, the Wards Island Walkway remains in the open position and is closed to pedestrians and cyclists.*)

A British outpost during the Revolutionary War, Wards Island traces its postwar roots back to a pair of brothers, Jasper and Bartholomew Ward, who set up a cotton mill here at the turn of the nineteenth century, and in 1807 built the City's first bridge over the East River to connect it to Manhattan. A drawbridge made entirely of wood, but for the two stone piers, the span lasted only fourteen years before it was annihilated by one of the only hurricanes in modern history to make landfall in New York City in 1821. Traffic to the island had already decreased after the Ward brothers closed the mill nineteen years earlier, but once the bridge went down, the island lay abandoned until 1840, when the City reinterred hundreds of thousands of remains here, exhumed, and transferred from Bryant and Madison Square parks, and turned it into a potter's field. The potter's field soon became a storage shed for the City's discarded and broken things. The island of junk became home to a poor house, an immigrant hospital, and an immigration depot, and for 150 years it has harbored some form of mental institution. In 1863, the New York City Asylum for the Insane opened as a male-only psychiatric hospital, admitting women to a separate facility on Blackwell's Island (currently Roosevelt Island) until 1892. Two years later, when the State took over caring for the mentally ill, patients from Blackwell's and Hart islands were resettled in the new coed Wards Island complex, and the name of the institution was changed to the Manhattan State Hospital for the Insane. Today, in addition to a city park and wastewater treatment plant (a running theme it seems in the City's less-fortunate neighborhoods), the island houses two asylums: the Manhattan Psychiatric Center—renamed from the former Manhattan State

Hospital—and the Kirby Forensic Psychiatric Center for the criminally insane fenced in behind barbed wire next door.

Ride around Wards Island Park, veering right at the fork in the road and the DO NOT ENTER **sign toward the Triboro/Robert F. Kennedy and Hell Gate bridges. Pass under the Triboro and wrap around the park to the left, away from Hell Gate** (a railroad bridge across the strait if the same name completed in 1917)**, staying right at the fork after climbing the short hill. At the wastewater treatment plant (the stop sign) turn left onto Ward Island Road, and follow it around until you reach the entrance to the pedestrian and cyclist's ramp to the Robert F. Kennedy Bridge on your left.**

Power up the ramp, leaving behind the twin psychiatric centers and the smokestack of the water treatment plant. The twin towers of the Triboro/Robert F. Kennedy rising ahead in the front of you.

Cross over the strait on the Triboro into the Queens neighborhood of Astoria. Traffic swirling by, on the roadway. (If your bike is heavy and you'd rather not carry it up and down the stairs, walk it up the wheel ramp the DOT was kind enough to install, or ride it up if you've got the legs for it.)

Astoria! Originally called Hallet's Cove after the first settlers here in 1659, William Hallet and his wife Elizabeth Fones, the 3.5-square-mile (9.1 km²) area is considered one of the most culturally diverse neighbor-

hoods on earth. Chartered and developed into a town in 1839, by Stephen Halsey, a fur trader from Manhattan by way of Flushing, Hallet's Cove was renamed Astoria in an attempt by Halsey to convince friend and fellow furrier John Jacob Astor (the richest man in the world at the time) to invest in his new planned community. Reportedly, Astor gave Halsey only $500 (a quarter of what he'd asked for), and declined an invitation to see the place, but Halsey named the town for him anyway. In all likelihood, he'd have done so even if Astor had given no money; the association to the famous tycoon alone helped to appropriate worth to the land.

As industry advanced and immigration increased, Astoria began layering itself with one ethnic group on top of another. The latter half of the nineteenth century brought Germans and Irish, including Henry E. Steinway (Heinrich Engelhard Steinweg), the exiled piano maker who founded Steinway and Sons. Italians began appearing in the 1920s, many expatriated from across the river from what even then was quickly turning into what is known today as Spanish Harlem. In the 1960s, with relaxed immigration laws, more Greeks began settling here than any other place in the world outside Greece and Cypress.

Today, while a sizeable Greek community still thrives here, along with the Italians, Germans, and Irish before them, Astoria appears to have become the City's welcome mat for new arrivals. From Hispanics to Arabs, Southeast Asians, Brazilians, Indians, and Bosnians to native Midwesterners and Californians, New York transplants first choose to live in Astoria because of its close proximity to Manhattan and more affordable housing market.

The neighborhood is also recognized for the various movie studios located here over the years, and for its numerous contributions to the film and television industry. Astoria Studio was one of the first, constructed in 1920 by Adolph Zuckor (founder of Paramount Pictures Corporation) during his Famous Players days. During WWII, after Zuckor moved Paramount to Hollywood and throughout the Korean War, the six sound stages of the studio were commandeered by the federal government and operated as the United States Army Pictorial Center, producing wartime propaganda and documentaries under the moniker of the Signal Corps Photographic Center. In 1970, the Army Pictorial Center was transferred to the Redstone Arsenal in Huntsville, Alabama, and the stages at Astoria Studio went largely abandoned until an NYC nonprofit organization brought them out of retirement to film *The Wiz*. After *The Wiz* production, the City approached commercial real estate developer George Kaufman to give the studio a much-needed face-lift, and in 1980, the now national historic landmark reopened as Kaufman Astoria Studios, or KAS as it is known today. Over the last three decades KAS, owned by NEP Broadcasting Company, has produced some of the world's most popular films and television shows, including, among others, the iconic *Sesame Street* and the 1980s breakthrough African American sitcom *The Cosby Show.*

Celebrity New Yorkers who've lived here? Broadway belter Ethel Merman, of "There's No Business Like Show Business" fame, grew up not far from Astoria Studio, and as a boy, Christopher Walken—*Deer Hunter, King of New York, Batman Returns, Pulp Fiction*—romped around his father's bakery at 30th and Broadway.

Come off the Triboro path at 27th Street and Hoyt Avenue. If you are thirsty or hungry, drop into the City's oldest beer garden (since 1910), **Bohemian Hall, at 29-19 40th Avenue between 31st and 29th streets,** for a chicken or pork schnitzel washed down with a Slovakian Golden Pheasant. Or, in true biker fashion, refuel with a Krusovice Dark,

an import from Czechoslovakia. **Otherwise, continue along Hoyt west to 21st Street and hang a left toward Astoria Boulevard, turning right onto Astoria. At 12th Street, veer right to stay on Astoria Boulevard and follow it to Eighth Street, turning left into the bike lane at Astoria Houses. Spin down Eighth Street and merge right with the bike lane onto Vernon Boulevard. The entrance to the Socrates Sculpture Park is approximately one thousand feet (305 meters) ahead on your right at the intersection of Broadway.**

From Socrates, continue on Vernon Boulevard toward the Queensboro Bridge, pedaling through Asthma Alley past the TransCanda (formerly Keyspan) oil and gas plant and the Queensbridge public housing projects on your way into Long Island City.

The birthplace of some of the biggest and most influential names in hip-hop, including NAS, Jay-Z, Roxanne Shanté, and pioneering producer Marley Marl, of the Juice Crew. In the shadow of the TransCanada (formerly Keyspan) triple smokestacks, complete with its own commercial district and 3,142 units sheltering nearly seven thousand people, Queensbridge Houses is the largest public housing project in North America.

From Queensbridge, spin under the 59th Street Bridge on Vernon to 45th Road and take a left. If you look to the east as you pass Queens Plaza South, you will see the massive neon Silvercup Studios sign, which used to mark the location of the Silvercup Bakery. Fifty years

ago, instead of oil, gas burn-off, and car exhaust from the bridge, 24/7, you would smell rack upon rack of fresh baked bread. Long Island City, a part of Queens, also boasts one of the biggest independent motion picture studios. Opened in 1983, in the flour silo of the former bread factory, Silvercup Studios has produced some of the industry's highest grossing as well as some of its most innovative and thought-provoking films and television series. Included among the award winners are Spike Lee's Golden–Globe honored *Do the Right Thing* and the nearly-hundred-million-dollar-earning Oscar-nominated *When Harry Met Sally,* the twice-crowned Best Drama *The Sopranos,* and the internationally syndicated *Sex and the City*.

Follow 45th Road across 11th Street past Murray Playground, named after Queens local and former parks recreation supervisor John F. Murray, **continuing through the light at 21st Street. When you reach the 7 Train platform, turn right onto 23rd Street.** If you decided against a snack back in *El Barrio,* or a stout or lager at the beer garden, the **Court Square Diner** to your right as you turn is among the best bargains the borough has to offer. Classic diner fare is served here. Nothing more, nothing less, and it's cheap! **From the diner, ride under the 7 Train tracks and wrap across Jackson Avenue as it becomes Davis Street. The 5 Pointz is approximately five hundred feet ahead on your right. PS1 is on Jackson, just to your right. You can see it from the corner.**

To return to Manhattan, or the Central Park starting point, from Davis Street and 5 Pointz, turn right (north) onto Jackson Avenue and follow it to Queens Boulevard. (Note: Traffic on Jackson Avenue is fairly heavy. Although the road and shoulder are wide enough to allow for safe riding, there is no designated bike lane here, so please remain careful and alert. In other words, this would not be a good time to text your girlfriend.) When you reach the stoplight at Queens Boulevard and the Queens Plaza subway overpass, Jackson Avenue becomes New York 25A. This is a tricky intersection. The safest way to cross it and turn onto Queens Plaza North, which leads you to the QB bike path entrance, is to cheat with the pedestrians and use the crosswalk. In other words, if you are unfamiliar with this area, get off your bike and walk under the overpass to the other side of Queens Boulevard. Once safely across, get back on your bike, wait for the light to change, then pedal across Jackson Avenue/New York 25A and veer to the right onto Queens Plaza North. At the traffic light, turn left and follow the plaza three blocks to Crescent Street until you see the signs for the QB bicycle entrance ahead on your left. Follow the signs and pedal onto the bridge. Although most cyclists ignore the stencils designating the pedestrian lane from bike lane, as of this writing, bicyclists are meant to share the lane left (or south) of the white dividing line. (Sometime in 2011, a new bike path will be completed along Queens Plaza North, making the route to the bridge easier to navigate.)

Opened on March 30, 1909, the Queensboro Bridge, also known as the 59th Street Bridge, was designed by Austrian immigrant, Gustav Lindenthal with input from Williamsburg Bridge draftsmen Leffert L. Buck and Henry Hornbostel. At approximately 7,450 feet in length (approach to approach), not only is the QB the longest of the four spans crossing the East River, but the grade up the ramp to the actual causeway—especially on the Manhattan side, climbing west to east—is also the steepest. And pencil-thin micro grooves cutting horizontally across the surface to slow your roll through the ascent make it feel even steeper.

Climb over the bridge made famous by Simon and Garfunkel in the "59th Street Bridge Song," otherwise known as "Feelin' Groovy." Stop when you reach the crest of the roadway and lean against the railing. Say hello to the lamppost and look down on Roosevelt Island, or out over the water to the north. The outlines of the Roosevelt Island, Triborough and Hell Gate bridges can be seen, looking dormant and silent like daytime carnival rides waiting for nightfall.

Originally called Hogs Island by the Dutch, then Blackwell's Island when the British took over and Robert Blackwell became the new Landlord, it underwent a third metamorphosis to Welfare Island before the powers that be finally settled on the present-day Roosevelt in 1972. The eel-shaped islet sprawled out in the middle of the East River seems to have had as many monikers as it has uses. Since 1832, after the City purchased it from the Blackwell heirs for $32,000, it has housed a penitentiary, two mental institutions, several hospitals, and today, in addition to the ruins of one of the country's first smallpox wards, the island is home to one of the City's newest residential developments. Notable past residents have included the late Al Lewis, who played "Grandpa" on the TV show *The Munsters,* as well as Ohio-born *Sex in the City* star Sarah Jessica Parker.

Initially planned as a car-free community (automobiles, roads, and buses have since been added), the island has only two modes of access: from Astoria, via the Roosevelt Island Bridge, or the Roosevelt Island Tramway, the first such form of transportation in the country, which connects the island to Midtown Manhattan.

Drop down from the QB and wrap around the bike lane back toward Roosevelt Island to the stoplight at 1st Avenue. Turn Left onto 1st Avenue, then left again onto East 61st Street. Follow 61st through the Upper East Side of Manhattan until it dead-ends at 5th Avenue and Central Park. Turn left on 5th, then right at light on 60th and veer to the right onto East Drive and follow it back to the starting point!

CHAPTER 5

BROOKLYN—CONEY ISLAND

(Fifteen Miles)

Narrioch

It's a typical summer day in Gotham. The sun high, the air wet and sluggish. Escape the unbearable heat of the City with a day trip to the land without shadows—*Narrioch* the native Lenape called it, also known as Coney Island. Where the sun will gleam no less hot, New Yorkers no less plentiful, but where else on the planet can you lie on the beach and go for a swim, have your photo taken with a sixteen-foot python named Shorty, shoot a paintball Uzi at a live human target in a game called *Shoot the Freak*, ride one of the oldest active Ferris wheels in the world, and enter an international hot dog eating contest all in the same afternoon?

Named for the abundance of rabbits that populated the long extinct woodlands here back in 1639, Coney Island morphed into a resort shortly after the American Civil War, when the *Coney Island and Brooklyn Railroad* streetcar line extended its tracks to the southernmost tip of Brooklyn.

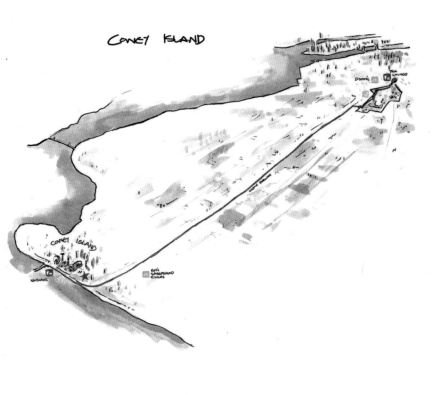

CONEY ISLAND

The first carousel was installed here in 1876, by Charles I. D. Looff, a Danish wood-carver, at the corner of West 6th Street and Surf Avenue, followed by the country's first roller coaster, the *Switchback*, in 1884. For eleven years, from 1885 until it was destroyed by fire in 1896, the *Elephant Hotel,* the island's first brothel, constructed in the shape of a colossal behemoth with windows, eclipsed the Statue of Liberty as the first sight masses saw upon arriving through the Narrows.

Sea Lion Park, the country's first permanent amusement park, was added in 1895, and by the turn of the 20th century after the Brooklyn Rapid Transit Company (BRT) converted the elevated train lines from steam power to the much faster electric, the resort had turned into a seaside getaway for less affluent day-trippers seeking to escape the City's overcrowded and stifling tenements.

Attracting millions of visitors annually in its prime, 1904 to 1911, Coney Island accommodated three competing amusement parks side by side: *Luna Park*, outlined in millions of novel electric lights; replacing the original *Sea Lion Park, Steeplechase Park,* and *Dreamland. Dreamland* offered its very own "Lilliputian Village," a cardboard city of three hundred midgets living in an experimental society, complete with its own legislature and fire department, as well as an exhibit of premature babies displayed in incubators monitored by registered nurses. Today the boardwalk is attempting to rise from the ashes of a century-long era of

decline and the ruins of a bitter development war. Although a modern-day version of *Luna Park*—sans light show—has been installed in the former location of Astroland (the last long-running major theme park to close its doors here in the fall of 2008), the new rides lack the novelty, invention, and danger of their predecessors. The Coney Island Freak Show presents an assortment of tattooed geeks, contortionists, and sword swallowers, but these days, when it comes to freaks and geeks, the everyday oddities and curiosities walking the boardwalk vie as much for our attention as those on stage. Fortunately, for the uninitiated, and those yearning for a dose of good ol' reliable past, a bit of the Astroland and Coney Island of yore remain in the legacy of the ninety-year-old Deno's Wonder Wheel, Nathan's Original Famous Frankfurters, and the Cyclone roller coaster. The coaster was designed and constructed in 1927, and is one of the oldest and most copied wooden roller coasters in the world still in operation.

The Ride

Begin at Grand Army Plaza, a gateway of concentric traffic circles heralding the entrance to the borough of Brooklyn's famed Prospect Park. Joining five major thoroughfares and the northwest neighborhoods of Prospect Heights and Park Slope, Grand Army Plaza celebrates yet another installment from nineteenth-century green space gurus, Frederick Law Olmsted and Calvert Vaux, and is home to a number of the City's cultural and historical landmarks. Among them are the *Soldiers' and Sailors' Memorial Arch* Civil War monument (designed by John H. Duncan,

future designer of Grant's Tomb), the central branch of the *Brooklyn Pub-lic Library,* and a year-round weekly farmers' market—one of fifty *Green-markets* sponsored throughout the City by Grow NYC. Attracting more than thirty local growers offering hundreds of varieties of organic, unpro-cessed, and free-range foods, the Greenmarket at Grand Army Plaza is the second-largest farmer's market in the City (behind Manhattan's Union Square), open every Saturday from eight o'clock in the morning to four in the afternoon.

From the Plaza, enter the park and merge onto West Drive. Formed some seventeen thousand years ago during the ebb of the Wisconsin gla-cial period, the 585-acre Prospect Park—bordered by Prospect Park West (9th Avenue), Flatbush and Ocean avenues, Fifteenth Street (Prospect Park Southwest), Parkside and Caton avenues—was once a heavily for-ested wilderness of hills and hollows. When Calvert Vaux took his drafting pencil to it (nearly 250 years and half a million residents later), the hills were still here, but the forest had given way to farmland and open pasture. Incorporating most of what remained of the natural topography into their vision for the park, a sweeping continuum of man-made meadows, hills, lakes, pools, waterfalls, and a wooded ravine billed as Brooklyn's last for-est, Olmsted and Vaux considered their sophomore effort superior to their first—Manhattan's venerated Central Park.

Like most of the City's green spaces, by the time the 1970s financial crisis steamrolled through town, Olmsted and Vaux's oasis in Greater New York's most populous borough had all but vanished. Although it had survived an 1869 neoclassical overlay of columns and the controver-sial Depression-era additions (the zoo, playgrounds, and postwar Woll-man Rink), the Ravine's Adirondack-inspired landscape and watercourse became eroded and clogged from decades of overuse and neglect. Finally, in 1994 with the aid of a batch of old photographs, postcards, and per-sonal essays, the recently formed Prospect Park Alliance came to the park's rescue; they embarked on a twenty-five-year-long painstaking mission to reconstruct Olmsted and Vaux's masterpiece. To date, with the planting of twenty thousand trees and shrubs and nearly 250,000 plants, not only has the Ravine been restored to its nineteenth-century splendor, but the slopes of the celebrated one-hundred-foot gorge have been cribbed and pegged to prevent future erosion.

Continue following West Drive around the park past the lake. The name changes here to West Lake Drive. Stay on West Lake until you see the exit sign for Ocean Parkway and Coney Island. In addition to Brooklyn's only forest and lake, hiking trails, and cycling paths, Prospect Park offers many other attractions and treasures including barbecue pits, a carousel for kids, a boathouse and Audubon Center, a horse stable, as well as the Picnic House and a dog pond. (You can find the pond somewhere between the Nethermead Arches and the entrance at 9th Street and 9th Avenue.)

If you drank too much coffee before the start, or sampled some of the fresh juices at the farmer's market and are in need of a restroom, there are two located just off West Drive at the Picnic House and Bandshell, at 5th and 11th streets. (Several others are located throughout, of course, should you decide to forgo the beach and hang out in the park for the day instead, but these are closest to the route). **Follow the signs for Coney Island and exit the park at Park Circle then wrap around the bike lane onto the east side of Ocean Parkway. Turn right at the second light onto Church Avenue, then left onto the tree- and bench-lined Greenway to pedal through the ambling neighborhood of Kensington.**

Kensington is one of Brooklyn's most diverse neighborhoods, presenting an array of housing styles as manifold as its people: from coops, to Victorians, to Cape Cods and Queen Annes, to brownstone row houses. Since 1885, after the construction of Ocean Parkway, the area has sheltered multiple communities of immigrants, and it is not uncommon to hear a minimum of fifteen different languages spoken within its 1.008-mile-square perimeter. Named after a district in England's West London, since 1930, the neighborhood has been home to Kensington Stables, one of only two remaining horse stables in Brooklyn, offering riding lessons for all ages and levels as well as guided equestrian tours through Prospect Park.

From Kensington, continue along the Greenway through Midwood—*Midwout,* or Middle Woods, as the Dutch called it. Though settled in 1652, the area remained rural and undeveloped until the completion of the parkway and the 1898 consolidation of Brooklyn, Queens, Manhattan, the Bronx, and Richmond (Staten Island) into the boroughs of Greater New York City. A primarily Jewish neighborhood, noteworthy residents have included Woody Allen, who grew up on the corner of Avenue K and Ocean Avenue and was a graduate of Midwood High School; world-renowned dramaturge Arthur Miller, who penned the Willy Loman every-man saga *Death of a Salesmen;* Lou Ferrigno, Dr. David Banner's alter ego in the TV series *The Incredible Hulk*; and Supreme Court Justice Ruth Bader Ginsburg. Aside from its celebrity-rich resident pool and popular-ity with filmmakers (the orderly tree-lined streets and manicured hedges and yards here have appeared in several movies, among them *The God-father* and *The Lords of Flatbush),* these days Midwood is a quiet, mostly orthodox neighborhood.

Separated from the walking path in 1894, the Greenway you are rid-ing was the country's first designated bike lane. Hundred-foot elm trees once lined this bikeway on both sides (in yet another offering by Olmsted and Vaux), until they became a breeding ground for the European bark beetle and died from Dutch Elm disease. Two five-and-a-half-mile walls of massive columnar trunks, like Doric pillars, capped by branches vault-ing over the center roadway like the ceiling in a great cathedral.

Here is New York.

See her as you ride. See her in the Hasidim, renewed from the Sabbath parading along the pedestrian path in *bekishes* and *sheit-els.* See her in the park goers resting on benches, in the backgam-

mon players and newspaper readers, eyes glued to their boards and pages. See her in the maintenance worker who keeps the path free of debris. Just past Avenue O, wedged between a mid-rise coop and a vacant lot, stands a rickety little frame house that looks like something out of a Brothers Grimm fairy tale. The resident is an elderly woman with ghost white hair, who is rumored to be crazy. All are the many faces of New York.

Continue on past Avenue O through Gravesend, chartered in 1643, by religious outcast and widowed British exile Lady Deborah Moody—the first woman in colonial America accorded a land patent. A fervent and persecuted Anabaptist who held that only believing adults should be baptized into the church, and established Gravesend as an oppression-free zone. Her land was the only English settlement in Dutch New Netherland, (one of the original six eventually consolidated into Kings County); she soon attracted a hodgepodge of religious followers. **If you care to make a slight detour here, turn right on Avenue U, then left on Van Sicklen Street, and pedal around the original historic square, turning left on Village Road South past the Old Gravesend Cemetery (which dates back to the mid 17th century). Purportedly, the lady herself is buried here in an unadorned unmarked grave somewhere. Cross McDonald**

Avenue and follow Village Road South to Village Road East, swinging left to Gravesend Neck Road. At Gravesend Neck, hang a right and ride back to Ocean Parkway. Turn right on OP and pick up the bikeway again at the next cross street, Avenue W, then continue to Coney Island and the boardwalk.

If for any reason you are in need of a bike shop, **Roy's Sheepshead Cycles** is just two blocks east at **2679 Coney Island Avenue and Avenue X.** Also, if you desire a bike shop at the beginning of the ride, **Dixon's is**

located two blocks from Grand Army Plaza at 792 Union between 6th and 7th avenues, across from the Tea Lounge—a great place to snack up before the ride as long as you don't mind baby strollers. (Several other bike shops are sprinkled throughout the vicinity of the route. For a complete listing, please see the "Coney Island Info Section" at the end of the chapter.)

When you are ready to return, simply follow the Ocean Park Greenway back to Park Circle and the park.

On The Wheel	
Name: Brendt Barbur **Age: 39**	
Occupation: Founding director, Bicycle Film Festival **Ride: Dahon Speed D7, Dahon Mu, Brazzo Road Bike, Cinelli Vigorelli Track, Ciocc Road Bike, S&M BMX**	

CHAPTER 6

FORT TILDEN/ROCKAWAY BEACH

(Thirty-five Miles)

Fort Tilden

Named in honor of Samuel J. Tilden, the twenty fifth governor of New York State, the yucca-, wormwood-, and rugosa-covered dunes of Fort Tilden State Park served as New York Harbor's first line of defense against hostile sea and air threats, along with Fort Hancock in New Jersey. From the dawn of World War I through the end of the Second World War, the former military base was armed with two sixteen-inch cannons known as Battery Harris. Their massive graffiti-tagged concrete encasements haunt the park's shore like the half-buried hulls of crash-landed alien spaceships. In the 1950s, the cannons were replaced with Nike anti-aircraft defense missiles, which were upgraded throughout the Cold War from *Hercules* to *Ajax*, until the weapons were deemed obsolete, and in 1974, the decommissioned base was handed over to the National Park Service as part of the Gateway National Recreation Area.

Located on the fingerlike prong of the Rockaway Peninsula, the fort's wild maritime flora are contrasted by the preserved missile silos and abandoned munitions buildings. Take advantage of the lookout points, offering stellar views of the Atlantic Ocean, Jamaica

Bay, and New York Harbor in the distance; a ride around the grounds yields an urban explorer's holy grail. Yet, hands down the biggest draw for New Yorkers and visitors willing to make the trek is the miles-long stretch of secluded beachfront snuggled between the dunes and the pristine (well, almost) waters of the Atlantic. If you are looking for a place to escape the throng, lie out naked on the sand (or not) and play in the surf, all without leaving the city, Fort Tilden is your beach. While it is slightly more crowded on weekends (emphasis on *slightly*, even during summer), weekdays the park is virtually deserted. Pack a lunch, a six-pack, plenty of sunscreen, a book, and any other essentials or supplies you feel you may need, as Fort Tilden is considerably off the beaten path. Also, there are no lifeguards here, so swim at your own risk.

In addition to the discarded armaments and tucked-away dune-protected seaside, the park also doubles as a center for the arts. Two of its jettisoned buildings and barracks have been transformed into studios for the Rockaway Artists Alliance—a nonprofit community arts organization that offers free lectures and exhibitions as well as mentoring and arts education to local youth. For the past twelve years another nonprofit, the Rockaway Theatre Company, has been presenting live theater in the former installation's 284-seat refurbished movie house. The company's season runs from the first weekend in June through Halloween. Rockaway Artist Alliance studios are open Saturdays and Sundays year-round from 12:00 noon to 4:00 PM.

Rockaway Beach

Seclusion and missile silos not your thing? The largest urban beach in the United States is only a five-mile spin east along the boardwalk. Once known as the City's Irish Riviera, this small sleepy community was initially settled as two villages, Holland and Hammel's, after the men who first purchased tracts of land here. Like Coney Island, Brighton, and the rest of the beach communities in New York, Rockaway's early years passed as a playground and retreat for the wealthy. But by the turn of the twentieth century, after Lewis Hammel relinquished some of his land for the peninsula's

first railway station, and after the completion of the first amusement park, *Rockaways' Playland* in 1901, the resort appeared on the radar of the City's less-fortunate masses and Rockaway Beach was soon reborn as an accessible and affordable day-trip and vacation locale.

In time, mostly Irish New Yorkers began opting for full-time residency on the peninsula and for the first half of the century, both resort and community thrived. Following trends throughout the rest of the City, after World War II, the neighborhood slid into decline. Even though two new bridges were constructed in an effort to facilitate automobile access for residents of Brooklyn and Queens, the Robert Moses era highway and other city improvement projects effectively isolated the small community. One of Moses's goals, since his 1920s appointment as chairman of the New York State Parks Department, was to construct a continuous oceanfront scenic drive from Staten Island all the way to the Hamptons. Had Robert Moses succeeded in building his Shore Front Parkway, the community would have been destroyed altogether. As it was, a number of residents were displaced anyway by the one and a half mile section Moses managed to complete before he was removed as head of the Triborough Bridge and Tunnel Authority (today's Metropolitan Transportation Authority). Homes not completely razed to make way for the "road from nowhere to nowhere," as locals call it, were cut in half. The parkway runs from Beach 109th Street to Beach 73rd. A number of the houses severed by it still stand.

Rockaway Beach though connected by a boardwalk is split into sections. Sixty seventh–69th and 87th–92nd streets are designated for surfers, while Jacob Riis Park and beaches further west are frequented by families, groups throwing parties, and festivals and sporting events like volleyball tournaments. During summer, lifeguards are on duty at all beaches from 10:00 AM to 6:00 PM, and bathrooms and snack stands are located at Jacob Riis. For a real treat, perhaps worth the entire ride out here, pedal down to 96th Street and Rockaway Beach Boulevard to Rockaway Taco for a Deluxe Fish Taco topped with homemade salsa. With DiCosmo's Home Made Italian Ice, Jack's Coffee, and the Organic Veggie Stand filling out the

rest of the corner, for the parched and famished, 96th and Rockaway is a magical bohemian snack shack oasis in a suburban desert of ticky-tacky.

The Ride

Option #1: Begin at the base of the Manhattan Bridge on the Brooklyn side at the corner of Jay Street and Sands. Follow Jay Street south (away from the water) toward Downtown Brooklyn to Tillery. Turn right onto Tillery and enter the bike lane. On Tillery, cross Adams Street and the entrance to the Brooklyn Bridge, then hang another right at the following light onto Cadman Plaza West. At the first intersection, turn left from Cadman (you can only turn left here) onto Clark Street to enter Brooklyn Heights. (If for some reason you are in immediate need of a bike shop, *Recycle a Bicycle* is just a few blocks toward the water in DUMBO at 35 Pearl Street, between John and Plymouth.)

Development of the country's first suburb began early in the nineteenth century, when steamboat pioneer Robert Fulton launched the City's first steam-powered ferry service between Manhattan and Brooklyn. The famous promenade was not here yet. Nor was the Brooklyn-Queens Expressway over which it is built. The automobile had yet to exist. With its vistas of the harbor and lower Manhattan, Brooklyn Heights began to appeal to the City's gentry, who preferred to come home to the calm and quiet promontory across the river. In the early twentieth century, after the Brooklyn Bridge was completed and an elevated line ran along old Fulton Street (now Cadman Plaza West), the neighborhood's resplendent views and close proximity to the shipyards and factories along the waterfront attracted everyone from dock workers, to prostitutes, to Jehova's Witnesses. Tenements even lined old Fulton Street for a time.

During the 1960s, Robert Moses began "improving" Brooklyn by taking a wrecking ball to the old world neighborhood on the bluff overlooking the East River and by replacing the buildings along Fulton Street with Cadman Plaza. Entire blocks of apartment buildings along the western boundary were leveled to make way for the automobile and the BQE.

Residents soon began to mobilize and, by 1965, had persuaded the newly formed Landmarks Preservation Commission to designate the neighborhood as the City's first historic district. Home at one time to Walt Whitman, Truman Capote, Bob Dylan, and Paul Giamatti (*Sideways* and *Cold Souls*), today, the Heights has undergone a regentrification of sorts. With town houses now selling for upwards of $10 million, it is safe to say that the privileged have returned.

If you wish to sightsee a bit before continuing on with the ride, a few of the landmarks saved by the commission include the Plymouth Church of the Pilgrims, on the corner of Hicks and Orange streets. It was established in 1847, by Henry Ward Beecher—abolitionist preacher and brother to *Uncle Tom's Cabin* author, Harriet Beecher Stowe. From Beecher's first service through the end of the Civil War, the church doubled as a prominent stop on the Underground Railroad. The 1839 town house in the basement of which Truman Capote wrote *Breakfast at Tiffany's* and *A House on the Heights* is located at 70 Willow Street, named, as you might imagine, for the willow trees that long ago lined the roadway. Word is that orchards once enveloped the area, with apple trees and plum trees, pears, peaches, and cherries, so abundant the branches had to be propped up to keep from breaking under the burden. The posh 1909 Bossert Hotel, one-time home to a number of Brooklyn Dodgers players, still towers at 98 Montague Street. In 1988, it was purchased and restored to original condition by the Jehovah's Witness Watchtower organization and used as a sort of dormitory for its members. In 2008, the Witnesses sold the former hotel for a reported $90 million. Today the historic building shelters luxury condominiums. Perhaps the most intriguing address in the Heights, and obviously there are many, is 58 Joralemon Street. A three-story nineteenth-century brownstone, with *Addams Family* black windows, that is not a brownstone at all. In fact, it is not even a house. Since 1908, it has been the façade of a not-so-secret emergency subway exit and vent building, owned by the Metropolitan Transit Authority (MTA). To take in some of the views that inspired so many to settle here, ride over to Columbia Heights and Pierrepont and check out the promenade. If you forgot to eat before you started out, *Lassen & Hennigs* at 114 Montague Street sells great sandwiches and cakes to go. For the vegetarian and vegan set, *Siggy's Good Food* is your spot at 76 Henry.

Follow Clark Street to Henry Street and turn left. Pedal through the Heights, then swing another left onto State Street. On State, ride three blocks to Court Street and turn right. Cross Atlantic on Court and breathe into Cobble Hill a couple of blocks, then bank left onto Dean Street into Boerum Hill.

Option #2: If you are itching to get out to the beach as soon as possible, and would rather bypass the bucolic exploration of America's first suburb, from Sands and Jay, follow Jay Street toward Tillary as in Option #1, only instead of turning when you reach Tillary Street, continue straight through the light on Jay and pass through Downtown Brooklyn. This option is extremely traffic and pedestrian dense, however, and virtually one giant exhaust pipe, so remain extra alert and careful here. Strapping on one those surgical masks might not be a bad idea either. Although there is a bike lane, it does little good here as cars and buses have essentially turned it into a parking lot, especially during the MTA shift change. After you cross Fulton, Jay Street turns into Smith Street, which turns one way the opposite direction at Schermerhorn. Turn left at Schermerhorn Street, then right onto Hoyt. Cross Atlantic on Hoyt Street and follow it to Dean.

Downtown Brooklyn is the third largest business district in the City behind Lower Manhattan and Midtown. The City of Brooklyn's Civic Center preconsolidation, when the borough was the fourth-largest city in the United States, boasts some of the borough's oldest nonresidential architecture. Borough Hall, at 209 Joralemon Street, from 1849 to 1898, was originally the city hall. Today, instead of the mayor's office, it houses the office of the borough president. The Federal Building and courthouse was completed in 1892 on a design by Mifflin E. Bell. The LMC designated the Romanesque revival structure a historic landmark in 1966. At 512 feet tall, the Williamsburgh Savings Bank clock tower (ahead in the distance as you turn onto Schermerhorn), is the second tallest building in Brooklyn behind the recently completed Brooklyner luxury condo tower at 111 Lawrence Street. For sixty years, until the Citibank building in Long Island City, Queens, eclipsed it, the old Williamsburgh Savings Bank at One Hanson Place was the tallest building on Long Island. At the time of its completion in 1929, it was the tallest four-sided clock tower in the world, and remains one of the loftiest today. In 2005, the landmark building was purchased by a group of developers including former NBA megastar, Magic Johnson, and converted into what else … ? Luxury condominiums. One block north at the corner of Ashland Place and Lafayette is the Brooklyn Academy of Music; that since 1908 has been presenting cutting-edge and genre-shaping performances of theater, dance, music, circus, and most recently cinema.

Turn left onto Dean Street into the neighborhood of Boerum Hill. Dissected and mythologized in acclaimed author Jonathan Lethem's novels, *Motherless Brooklyn* and *Fortress of Solitude*, Boerum Hill is home to the City's only remaining cornfield. Okay, corn patch may be more accurate. On the corner of Smith and Bergen streets tucked away on the sidewalk in front of the subway entrance and Domino's Pizza, so small and discreet you might miss it unless you are walking or traveling by bicycle, is a raised-bed garden of blue flint corn, squash, and beans. The garden was conceived and planted in the spring of 2010 by artist and filmmaker Christina Kelly as an art project and daily reminder of what once was, and how drastically things have changed since then. Four hundred years ago the region of Brooklyn bordered by Court Street, Schermerhorn, 4th Avenue, and Warren Street, known as Boerum Hill, was a native planting ground in the *Lenape* village of *Marechkawikingh.* Even after the Dutch arrived in 1646, changing the name of the village to *Breuckelen*, the area remained farmland and otherwise undeveloped until the mid-nineteenth century. In fact, most of the row houses and brownstones you are passing were built between 1840 and 1870, and from the mid-1800s to the turn of the century, Boerum Hill evolved into a primarily middle-class neighborhood populated by traders and craftspeople. Named after Simon Boerum, whose family was the first of the European settlers to farm the land here. As the merchants and artisans amassed their fortunes and moved to swankier neighborhoods, the hill once again was inhabited by Indians. Mohawks this time, steelworkers from Canada, beckoned to the City by the new skyscraper and bridge building craze. After World War II, the Mohawks headed west, and chunks of the neighborhood were demolished to make way for Gowanus Houses, one of Robert Moses's urban renewal schemes. A fourteen-complex housing project crammed between Wyckoff, Douglas, Hoyt, and Bond Streets. Along with the row houses razed, the neighborhood also lost its name, becoming known for a time simply as Gowanus or South Brooklyn. In the 1990s (a.k.a. the zero tolerance years), the nineteenth-century row houses and brownstones of Boerum Hill, as well as the old name, were rediscovered and restored. In addition to Lethem's literary treatment of the tree-lined neighborhood, renowned filmmaker Spike Lee's 1995 crack and street gang drama *Clockers* was shot in Gawanus Houses. The year before the film was released, the acetate-engraved housing project was the scene of the widely publicized murder of Nicholas Heyward Jr. the thirteen-year-old boy shot by a police officer who mistook the toy gun he was brandishing during a cops and robbers game for a real one.

Continue on Dean Street through Prospect Heights to Bedford. Bike shops in the area include *Bicycle Station* at 171 Park Avenue between Carlton and Adelphi, and *Brooklyn Bike and Board* at 560 Vanderbilt between Dean and Bergen Streets.

Often overshadowed by the park and its wealthier neighbor Park Slope, Prospect Heights is one of the borough's oldest neighborhoods, as well as one of the City's newest historic districts. Designated a landmark in 2009, like Boerum Hill through which you just passed, many of the 850-some odd buildings puckered between Atlantic Avenue, Eastern Parkway, Washington Avenue, and Flatbush Avenue number among the borough's oldest. The neighborhood was named for the hill it surrounds, which in turn was named for the immense and striking views it once afforded, enabling the looker to see to the west all the way to New Jersey and east as far as Long Island. Originally formed by the same glacier that carved the rest of the borough's wooded hillsides and valleys, as the second highest peak in Brooklyn (behind Battle Hill in Greenwood Cemetery), Mount Prospect served its country as the Continental Army's lookout point during the Revolutionary War Battle of Long Island.

In addition to the historic row houses and landscape, Prospect Heights also harbors its share of important cultural institutions including the Brooklyn Museum, the Brooklyn Botanic Garden, and the main branch of the Brooklyn Public Library, in what was once referred to as the Institute Triangle. Conceived in 1890, it would have been the largest museum structure in the world had it not been for consolidation and lackluster funding that was only able to construct a portion of the original plan. Among the more than a million and a half objets d'art, housed in the Beaux-Arts building's 560,000 square feet of space, is one of the world's finest Egyptian art collections, as well as sculptor Daniel French's massive seated Ms. "Brooklyn" and "Manhattan" statues. The statues once held court at the Brooklyn end of the Manhattan Bridge, until their thrones were destroyed in a 1963 bridge improvement project, orchestrated, of course, by none other than our own Robert Moses. The belle of the fifty-acre botanic garden is the Cherry Walk, whose Japanese cherry trees, in bloom the last two weeks of April, rival their more famous sisters in the nation's capital.

For the past seven years, in what some might call a modern-day Battle of Brooklyn, the overlooked neighborhood has been embroiled in controversy. That seven-block-long gaping hole in the ground, one street over to your east (between Pacific Street and Atlantic Avenue, from Flatbush Avenue to Vanderbilt), represents the latest example of the City exercising its right of eminent domain—the right of a government or agency to seize private property, with compensation, for public use—on behalf of a private developer. In this case, the developer is Forest City Ratner, a division of Cleveland, Ohio-based developer Forest City Enterprises. In 2003, under the umbrella of eminent domain, Forest City Ratner, who was also part of a group that acquired the New Jersey Nets National Basketball Association franchise, announced its plans to demolish the properties it had purchased and build a new professional sports arena to house the Nets in their place. The site would also accommodate sixteen high-rise condominiums, and rental and office towers, in the heart of what has come to be called Brownstone Brooklyn. In addition to the residential and commercial properties, the developer also obtained the Long Island Rail Road yard that runs along the same tract of land, also known as the Vanderbilt Yard. The project as originally proposed would have cost $4.9 billion dollars and occupied twenty-two acres of real estate. As it stands now, after seven years, twelve lawsuits (filed and lost by Prospect Heights residents associations opposed to the project), the removal of the original architect, and a collapsed economy, only the arena, and possibly one of the office towers, is slated for construction. For now, the residential towers, meant to replace the housing that was expropriated, has been scrapped. When the rest of the hole will be filled is entirely up to FCR, which, according to the fine print in the official approval documents, has twenty-five years to complete its project.

It has been said that every twelve years New York becomes a different city. That even with all the protection, the designating of landmarks, and residential districts historic, the New York of yesteryear, whatever the year, is no longer recognizable in the New York of today. Time and again we return to the neighborhoods that shaped our childhoods, or college years, or first few weeks as transplants in this city, and we are all transplants from one time or place or another, only to find that although our old sublet may remain, the corner store is now a sixty-story condo complex, and the local pizza joint has given way to a trendy gourmet coffee shop that serves $5 glasses of organic milk with $8 peanut butter and jelly sandwiches. In many cases, even the name of the neighborhood has changed. SoHo to NoLita. Hell's Kitchen to Clinton. The Wholesale district to NoMad. Boerum Hill to South Brooklyn and back to Boerum Hill again. *Marechkawikingh* to *Breuckelen. Manahatta* to Manhattan. *Nieuw Amsterdam* to New York. It is an old story, as old as the City itself, and the reason so many are drawn here: to remake ourselves in the city that every twelve years has been remaking itself for centuries.

So, before Prospect Heights shape-shifts into Barclay Center Flats (after the name of the new arena), some places and events worth checking out while they are still here include the LAVA Studio at 524 Bergen Street between Carlton and 6th Avenue. LAVA is a nonprofit dance, theatre, and acrobatic performance troupe. For eleven years running, LAVA has been a fixture in the local community, teaching and training Prospect Heights residents and beyond in the company's "rigorous, creative, and inclusive movement language." Classes are offered spring and fall, to both children and adults from beginners to advanced; and every spring members of the community are invited to participate in the studio's annual Handstand-a-Thon to help raise money for scholarships awarded to neighborhood children otherwise unable to afford classes. Labor Day weekend, Prospect Heights plays host to the annual West Indian Day Parade, the largest parade in the City, celebrating Caribbean peoples and culture. Every year, millions of New Yorkers from all five boroughs line up along the Eastern Parkway to applaud the brightly-colored spectacle, bask in the late summer sun, dance to the infectious beats and consume as much jerk chicken and fried flying fish as their stomachs allow.

At Bedford, turn right into the bike lane and enter Crown Heights.

Once part of the Bedford Hills, a range of "Green Mountains" that ran from Battle Pass in Prospect Park along Eastern Parkway, including Mount Prospect, all the way east to Long Island, picking up across the Sound and continuing on to Oyster Bay. The neighborhood sprawled between Prospect Heights, Prospect-Lefferts Gardens, Bedford-Stuyvesant (Bed-Stuy), and Brownsville was originally called Crow Hill for all the crows that used to flock to a nineteenth-century bone factory located here. As recent as the Revolutionary War, the entire chain of hills was still wooded, and the neighborhood was not awarded its present-day moniker of Crown Heights until 1916, when Crown Street was cut through from Rochester to Washington Avenue.

Although West Indians, Jamaicans, and Black Americans began arriving in the 1920s, through the first half of the century Crown Heights remained predominantly white and Jewish. The Chabad-Lubavitch Hasidic movement established its world headquarters here. By the 1960s, those demographics began to change. As the Civil Rights Movement gained momentum, and racial tensions flared throughout the country, Crown Heights became a volatile environment to which few, in hindsight, were paying close attention. While most of the white population fled the neighborhood for less strained environs, the Lubavitch community elected to stay. With continuing immigration from the West Indies and Jamaica, overnight Crown Heights' demographics went from roughly 90 percent white to 90 percent black. Inflaming the already-explosive environment, economically, the 1970s financial crisis sent the neighborhood to the brink, distinguishing Crown Heights as one of the poorest residential districts in the country. The different cultural factions grew increasingly suspicious of one another, and were looking for someone to blame for their impoverished plight; fate provided the neighborhood an answer on the evening of August 19, 1991.

At approximately 8:20 PM, twenty-two-year-old Lubavitch member Yosef Lifsh was driving west on President Street as part of Chabad-Lubavitch leader Rabbi Menachem Mendel Schneerson's three-car motorcade. What happened next is still up for debate. While some witnesses insisted that Lifsh ran a red light, others recounted that the light was yellow. In either case, as he entered the intersection of President and Utica, he collided with another vehicle. In a freak and catastrophic accident, the station wagon Lifsh was driving bounced off the other car, careened onto the sidewalk, and killed seven-year-old African American Gavin Cato, who had been walking there with his cousin Angela. Angela survived, but suffered a broken leg. Tragic as it was, the accident was merely the match that lit the fuse, and legitimate or not, the neighborhood's black community finally had a face to blame for all its ills. Its visage was white and Jew-ish, and it was going to pay. In what many have called an unprecedented act of American anti-Semitism, three hours after the accident a group of angry black youths jumped and stabbed to death a visiting Orthodox Aus-tralian Jewish scholar on his way home, named Yankel Rosenbaum. The calamitous events of that evening kicked off a three-day riot that shook the City to its core. By the time the violence was quashed, in addition to the deaths of Cato and Rosenbaum nearly 200 people were injured (150 of them police officers), 130 rioters were arrested, and the property damage to businesses and vehicles was estimated at over a million dollars.

In the aftermath, the neighborhood and residents eventually recov-ered—the Hasidim and blacks learned to reconcile, a number have even attempted to identify common ground. With new arrivals to the City and forced-out Manhattanites scouring the outer boroughs for affordable hous-ing, Crown Heights today is far from the poverty-stricken hotbed it was when the riots broke out; in fact, as a rediscovered "up and coming" part of historic brownstone Brooklyn, its vintage housing stock is well on the rise. The 1890 Richardsonian Romanesque building across the street, for example, on the corner as you turned right from Dean onto Bedford, was once home to the Union League Club of Brooklyn, the Republican Party's premier social hotspot. Today it serves the needs of Bed-Stuy's and Crown Heights' elders as the Bhraggs Grant Square Senior Citizens' Center. Even would-be celebrities are reclaiming the hood. The two-mile square block of streets that gave us Shirley Chisholm, the nation's first black congress-woman, and Susan McKinney Steward, New York's first black female phy-sician, is now home to DeScribe (pronounced *Dee*-Scribe), the neighbor-hood's first Hasidic rapper. But even from the far-removed vantage point of time, the air of both the tragedy and the conditions leading up to it still lingers. It doesn't take much effort to feel it as you ride. A heightened sense of alertness washes over you, a tightening of the muscles, the unexplained urge to pedal a little faster and maybe not be so quick to rail at the driver of the SUV parked in the bike lane. It's nothing tangible, really. Nothing you can see, just a leftover odor of something. A thing unsettled.

Continue south on Bedford through Prospect-Lefferts Gardens. Just past Eastern Parkway, the bike path surface turns a bit bumpy here and remains so all the way out to Sheepshead Bay. Lefferts Gardens was named after James Lefferts, a nineteenth-century merchant and descendent of one of the City's oldest families, who in 1893 carved up the family estate into six hundred property lots and sold them off to middle-class New Yorkers. This allowed the New Yorkers to construct single family homes of brick or stone at least two stories tall. The instant neighborhood sprouting up across the newly created lots like brick and mortared Chia Pets˙ was called Lefferts Manor.

In the historic section that still bears the name, between Flatbush Avenue, Rogers Avenue, Fenimore Street, and Lincoln Road, the original building covenant is still in force, and riding through it, should you choose to take a detour, is a bit like traveling back to a time. To a place when the boroughs of Greater New York still resembled the rest of America's checkerboard landscape of drowsy towns miles and miles from the hustle of the big city. Today Lefferts Manor has been folded into the larger neighborhood of Prospect-Lefferts Gardens, which extends from Empire Boulevard south to Clarkson Avenue, from Ocean Avenue, or Prospect Park, east to New York Avenue. For another quick diversion, you can visit the Lefferts family home (now a museum), located inside the park by the zoo at the intersection of Empire Boulevard, Flatbush, and Ocean avenues. **This is also a good place to stop and use the restroom, if needed, as comfort stations are available at the Flatbush/Ocean Avenue entrance, as well as the Lincoln Road Playground, one block south on Ocean Avenue.**

From Lefferts Gardens… you guessed it, stay on Bedford as you spin through Flatbush-Ditmas Park. Bedford narrows into a bumpy two way, two-lane street here, and it is a rather long ride in general, so slipping into a pair of padded bike shorts before you start might not be a bad idea. Also, the bike lane runs too close for comfort to the row of parked cars along the side, so give yourself a wide berth and ride as close to traffic as feels safe for you to keep from getting doored.

From Church Avenue to Avenue H, from Bedford Avenue to Coney Island Avenue, Ditmas Park is another of the Flatbush historic districts, designated so for all the run-down, mostly turn-of-the-century stand-alone bungalow style, Colonial Revival, and neo-Tudor houses—with full-length porches no less—that populate the elm-lined streets here. Once home to the wealthy, today Ditmas Park residents run the gamut of color schemes and cultures, including West Indians, Hasidim, immigrants from India, as well as college students, artists, and hipsters taking advantage of the large humane living spaces and relatively inexpensive rents. For food options, the not-so-cheap Flatbush Food Coop is located at 1318 Cortelyou Road between Marlborough and Rugby. In fact, Cortelyou is the place for all your break-from-the-ride needs in this neighborhood, from delis to coffee shops, bars, and full-scale restaurants. Just don't expect it to be cheap.

Careful at the intersection of Flatbush. It's not exactly a jog around, but it feels like one, and traffic is fairly dense here. At Avenue H, pedal between the ivy-covered buildings and campus of Brooklyn College on your way through the cookie-cutter-style Dutch farm-houses of Midwood. (For Midwood history, neighborhood attractions, etc., please

see the Midwood section in the Coney Island ride.) The merger of the Downtown Brooklyn campus of Hunter College (at the time still women only) and the BK branch of City College of New York (men only) created Brooklyn College in 1930 as the first coed liberal arts school in the City. The cornerstone for this campus was laid in 1936, and except for the ivy crawling over the façades of a number of the prewar architecture, much of it looks the same as when the first students began enrolling here. Famous alumni of the college include actor Michael Lerner; *Outlaw* costar Jimmy Smits; Daniel Keyes, author of the award-winning classic novel *Flowers for Algernon;* and Sapphire, author of the acclaimed best-selling novel *Push,* which was the inspiration for the movie *Precious.*

From Brooklyn College and Midwood, take a deep breath as you head into Sheepshead Bay and see if you can smell the salt in the air from the ocean. When you reach the water, turn left onto Emmons Avenue. Follow Emmons along the water to Brigham Street. Make a quick jog right, then left at the Dead End sign at Brigham onto the bike path, continue on east parallel to the roadway. (If you pass Knapp Street and the NO LEFT TURN sign, with the big green BELT PARKWAY—EAST, PASSENGER CARS ONLY warning a short distance ahead in the background, you've gone too far and will need to double back on the sidewalk a block or so to return to Brigham. In this case you will be turning left, left to pick up the bike lane.) Remember, the bike lane is also a shared pedestrian pathway, so be sure to practice good bike etiquette and give a warning before you pass.

Originally known as the cove, in many ways Sheepshead Bay is not unlike many other salty dog harbor towns. Gray-haired men with gold watches and permanently tanned leather skin camp on lawn chairs on the sidewalk under patches of too little shade and smoke cigars and stare at the fishing boats docked at port. For some reason the sky always seems bigger at the sea, bluer, and the sun hotter. Seafood restaurants and tackle and bait shops line the shore. Veil-thin wisps of clouds whisper through all that blue as though trying to disguise their presence. The bay is named for a fish, once plentiful in the waters here.

As usual, nineteenth-century wealthy Manhattanites were the first to develop the cove as a resort, when they stayed at the hotels and gambled at the casinos at Manhattan and Brighton Beaches opposite on the southern shore. Prior to that until the late 1800s, the neighborhood was tilled as farmland. Before the farmers settled in, the Canarsee Indians fished for sheepshead here (hence the name), a thick striped or banded fish that rarely reaches more than eight inches in length, and looks like its body has been sandwiched between the jaws of a vise. These days, pollution has pushed the sheepshead to southern waters, and though the name remains, they can no longer be found here.

Not too long after the businessmen and traders from Manhattan arrived, a racetrack was installed. From 1880 to 1911, until the State of New York temporarily outlawed *pari-mutuel* track betting (pool wagering), the Sheepshead Bay Racetrack was known for originating two races: the Suburban Handicap and the Futurity Stakes. When the Futurity was run for the first time in 1888, it was the richest race in the land. Today, part of the old racetrack is buried under a the foundation of a Duane Reade Pharmacy and attendant parking lot (the rest has been erased by housing). Other than the fishing boat rentals, the Rockaway Inlet bay is probably best known for its annual Bayfest celebration, a free all-day festival with music, amusement rides, games, sailing demonstrations, prize giveaways, and free boat rides. In its twenty-first year, Bayfest kicks off every May 15 from noon to 6:00 PM, rain or shine. To date, it is New York City's only vendor-free street fair. Like every other New York neighborhood, it seems, Sheepshead Bay has raised its share of celebrities. Most notable, perhaps, is NPR Fresh Air host Terry Gross. If you must eat, Randazzo's is rumored to have the best clam bar around. The secret, apparently, is in the sauce.

Follow the bike path until it turns into an inch-deep quagmire of dirt and sand. At this point, you have two options. You can cycle up and power through it, easiest on a mountain bike, but doable on a road, fixed or single speed as well. Or, you can get off and walk the hundred yards or so until it dead-ends at a parking lot. Either way, don't forget to look to your right for a great view of the inlet and Lower New

York Bay. Ride through the parking lot another thirty yards until you reach the porta potties and hot dog truck. If you've no need to use the bathroom, or stop for a snack break, veer around the front of the hot dog truck to pick up the bike path again.

Continue on the path, heading east, and follow the Belt Parkway bridge over the channel leading into Deep Creek and Dead Horse Bay. Spin along the pathway through Brooklyn Marine Park, following the arrows and veering to the right until it dumps you out on Flatbush Avenue. Shadow Flatbush on the path until you reach the first traffic signal. Cross Flatbush with the light, then pick up the path on the other side of the roadway and cycle along the path past Floyd Bennett Field.

The City's first municipal airport, the runways at Floyd Bennett Field officially opened to commercial air traffic in 1931. Since 1972 the airport has no longer been operational and the field now serves as part of the Gateway National Recreation Area, offering a range of events and activities free to the public, including Ecology Village, the City's only overnight campground, with big black open skies perfect for stargazing; a museum of historic "nose hangars" in which 1950s era aircraft are on display for public viewing; and from the beginning of May through the end of August, the Kissena Cycling Club sponsors the Tuesday Night Race Series. A circuit race season on a 2.3-mile course over the field's abandoned windswept and weatherworn runways, organized by former professional racer Charlie Issendorf. Participants must be licensed and pay an entry fee of $20. Yellow jerseys are awarded in the overall points category as well as green jerseys for sprints.

Ride along the bike lane past Floyd Bennett to the traffic light at Aviation Road, cross back to the other side of Flatbush, pick up the path, and cross over Jamaica Bay via the Marine Parkway Gil Hodges Memorial Bridge. Once again, the bridge pathway is a narrow shared bike and pedestrian lane. So go slow, shout out the appropriate warning when passing, and be prepared to stop, if necessary, and lean against

the railing to allow riders to pass in the opposite direction. At the bottom of the bridge, wrap around to the right onto the pathway, then hop the curb onto Rockaway Point Boulevard/State Road and follow the bike lane to the traffic light and entrance to Fort Tilden State Park. Cross Rockaway Point at the light (left), and enter the park.

Welcome to Fort Tilden!

To access the beaches, follow the entrance road past the kiosk (on your right) to the stop sign and turn right. (For point of reference, when you reach the stop sign, there should be a chapel directly across the street from you, as well as a sign board with directional arrows pointing you to the various sections of the park.) Once you make the turn, a comfort station will be located to your right, if you are in need of a restroom. Pass

the building and the ensuing parking lot on your left. At the end of the parking lot, turn left past the ROCA bunkers. Pedal through the remainder of the parking lot until you come to the end, then veer onto the blocked-off road to the right. The road should only be closed to vehicles; bikes have plenty of room to maneuver around the barricades. At the NO LEFT TURN and stop signs, turn left and follow the fence-lined path toward the water until it dead-ends at the dunes, then turn right (you can only turn right here). After turning, the beaches will be to your left, just over the sand dunes. As you follow along the pathway, you will begin to see makeshift ramps every fifty yards or so, guiding you over

the dunes to one of the beaches. Pick one, and enjoy. Remember, the farther west you go, the more secluded the beach. To secure your bike, if it is a beater, you may either lock it to the chain-link fence or to one of the street signs across from the ramps on the dune path. If your bike is your de facto girlfriend, as is the case with the authors of *Bike NYC*, and you want to ensure nothing happens to it (this is New York City after all), we recommend taking it with you onto the beach.

To Return

From Fort Tilden, simply retrace your route through the park back to the Marine Parkway Bridge and return the way you came.

From Rockaway Taco, follow 96th Street north to Beach Channel Drive and take a left. Follow Beach Channel Drive along Jamaica Bay all the way back to the Marine Parkway Bridge and return the way you came. You may also return along the boardwalk, if you desire more time at the beach.

CHAPTER 7

RUMBLE THROUGH THE BRONX

(Twenty Miles)

THE BRONX

Home to the twenty-seven-time world champion New York Yankees baseball team, the world-renowned Bronx Zoo and New York Botanical Garden, as well as the largest park and wetlands the City has to offer, the Bronx is the only one of the five boroughs physically connected to the North American mainland. The City's northernmost county takes its name from the Bronx River, which in turn was named after Jonas Bronck, a seventeenth-century immigrant from Sweden and the area's first non–Native American settler. Slow to develop, the Bronx remained largely rural until the first elevated train arrived, followed by the City's new subway system, linking the borough to Manhattan in 1904; this convenient form of public transporation induced a period of astonishing growth. In the first three decades of the twentieth century, the second smallest borough's population mushroomed to six times its size, from 200,000 inhabitants in 1900 to 1.3 million by the 1930s. Italian and Irish immigrants arrived first, escaping the overcrowded conditions on the Lower East Side, along with

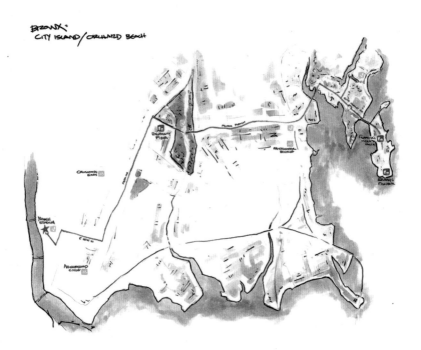

BRONX:
CITY ISLAND/ORCHARD BEACH

Germans and a Jewish community that by 1937 totaled nearly 45 percent of the population.

After Word War II, as Puerto Ricans, Dominicans, and American blacks began moving into the borough (particularly the neighborhoods South of 183rd Street and West of the Bronx River), the Bronx saw an unparalleled stampede of Caucasian people fleeing, during the 1940s through the 1960s, to counties father north and in some cases down south to retirement villas in Florida. The departure—on top of the racial tensions, financial implosion, and crime wave capsizing the rest of the City, as well as destructive and what many believe intentional government policies targeted at the South Bronx and Harlem in particular—left a crater-sized hole in the borough, both literally and figuratively, that the city has only recently begun to fill.

In addition to the construction of Robert Moses's Cross Bronx Expressway, which destroyed 113 blocks of working-class neighborhoods, displacing thousands of residents, while preserving more affluent enclaves north and west, beginning in the 1960s, infrastructure—from banks and insurance companies to grocery stores, police, fire, and garbage services—completely abandoned the South Bronx in what has since become known as the twin practices of "redlining" and "planned shrinkage," in an attempt to force the poor to camp out on some other municipality's doorstep, freeing up the valuable commodity of real estate in this city to be redeveloped into environs more pleasing to Gotham's eye. To devastate the community even further, landlords turned their backs on rent-controlled apartment buildings (read: unprofitable), letting them fall into horrible disrepair; and several, it is believed, jettisoned the properties from the sinking ship altogether. In the 1970s, a rash of fires, all in the South Bronx and all deliberately started, turned the already-ravaged landscape into the aftermath of a battle zone, something reminiscent of a war-torn wasteland. Only those too poor to move remained. By the early 1990s, the South Bronx population had been reduced to fewer than 6,000 residents.

Today—in a two runs down, bottom of the ninth, two outs and the Babe at the plate, Yankee-style comeback—while still home to one of the poorest congressional districts in the country, after reeling in free fall for over three decades, the South Bronx knocked one out of the park, and once again the borough's population numbers nearly 1.4 million residents. Led by the grassroots efforts of community groups like the Bronx Center Project, whose motto is "Don't Move, Improve," and Nos Quedamos, meaning "We Stay" in Spanish. Neighborhood church groups took matters into their own hands, and as of 2007, nearly $5 billion of both private and public money has been spent, mostly in the South Bronx, to bring this borough back to life.

From the old Yankee Stadium to Pelham Bay Park and Orchard Beach, from the South Bronx to City Island, we take you on a ride to sample the texture of some of the neighborhoods and residents that make up the storied borough which, perhaps more so than others, have done what New Yorkers do best—survive and overcome, no matter how stacked the odds.

THE RUMBLE

Begin at the Big Bat, the 138-foot-tall exhaust pipe painted to look like Babe Ruth's legendary baseball bat, the Louisville Slugger, **at the main entrance to Heritage Field Park (fall 2011), former site of the old Yankee baseball stadium at the junction of East 153rd and 157th streets.** *Note: Bike shops are a bit scarce in the Bronx, especially out toward City Island and Pelham Bay, so make sure to bring everything you'll need to fix a flat or make a quick repair (spare tube, patch kit, tire irons, Allen*

keys, small adjustable wrench and screwdriver). **If you find yourself in need of a shop at the start, however, Neighborhood Cycle is at 571 Courtlandt Avenue on the corner of East 150th Street.**

Christened "The House that Ruth Built" by twentieth-century New York–based sportswriter Fred Lieb, the first Yankee Stadium in which the Babe hit the majority of his 714 career home runs was completed in 1923, four years after the New York franchise purchased the Hall of Fame slugger from its American League rival, the Boston Red Sox. The first sports facility in the country officially titled a "stadium" as opposed to a field, grounds, or ball yard, the Yankees' new home was also the first with triple-deck seating, accommodating a record—at the time—58,000 fans. From opening day in 1923 until the final game on September 21, 2008, in addition to hosting thirty-seven World Series (of which the Yankees won all but 11), the stadium underwent a massive $100 million renovation and held thirty championship boxing bouts including Joe Louis's 1938 symbolic and historic knockout of the German Max Schmeling and the 1976 15-round Muhammad Ali–Ken Norton decision, one of the rope-a-dope champ's last titles. The stadium also fielded an unsuccessful professional football team, also called the Yankees; doubled as a soccer stadium from 1931 to 1976; hosted religious conventions, rock concerts, and three separate masses celebrated by three different popes; and witnessed a wedding.

Today the eighty-five-year-old stadium has been demolished, replaced by a younger, hipper twenty-first-century model across the street that looks a lot like the old one. In the fall of 2011, Heritage Field Park will open on the site of the former Yankee Stadium, surrounded by three complimentary parks, one atop a parking garage, returning forty acres of green space the new stadium displaced. The bat will remain as a symbol and reminder of the history made here, but the land and nearby blighted real estate will be converted to state-of-the-art outdoor recreational facilities that include amateur soccer, football, and baseball fields; a running track; walkways; grass berms; basketball, handball, and tennis courts; and a skateboard park. The ball fields and the basketball and handball courts are to be shared by Public School 29 and the surrounding community.

Pedal southeast on East 153rd and turn left on River Avenue. Ride on River Avenue under the 4 train tracks to East 161st Street and turn right onto East 161st. Follow 161st to Melrose Avenue and spin left into the bike lane. Traffic can be congested on 161st Street, but it's totally rideable and only lasts a few blocks. Remember your mantras: Stay visible and keep four feet clearance between you and the parked cars to avoid the proverbial door.

Among the hardest hit in the assault on poverty and the neighborhood's poor, Melrose Commons has become the poster child for the South Bronx's renewal. Established in the 1850s as a German village—with shops, movie theaters, burlesque houses, delis and bakeries—by the time the borough's population hit the one million mark, Melrose Avenue was known as the Broadway of the Bronx. After the fires and withdrawal of services to the area, in 1992, purely by accident, the five hundred or so residents and business owners left in the burned-out neighborhood got wind of a City-sponsored urban renewal plan, nine years in the making, to evict them all and then unleash the wrecking balls on what remained of their homes and storefronts in order to make way for a new 2,600-unit middle-class devel-

opment complex. Refusing to go without a fight, and with the help of the Bronx Center Project, Melrose residents formed a neighborhood coalition called Nos Quedamos (We Stay) to fight the plan. After teaching themselves how to navigate the murky and turbulent waters of city government, consulting with independent design and architectural firms, while holding literally hundreds of meetings over a period of six months, Nos Quedamos convinced the City to scrub its original plan in favor of its own, which not only saved the residents'

homes and businesses, but also addressed serious sustainability, environmental, and health issues.

Although the founder and original executive director of Nos Quedamos, Yolanda Garcia, passed away in 2005 (her daughter, also named Yolanda, heads the group now), to date, the coalition has spearheaded the completion or near completion of sixteen new buildings (a number of which you are riding past right now)—including over 2,400 new apartments or condos, retail space, and a community college campus—with hundreds more on the way. The coalition also made similar developments in neighboring Morrisania and East Tremont. Perhaps when the project is all said and done, they will be nicknamed "The Homes that Yolanda Built"!

Ride north on the Melrose bike lane until it merges with Park Avenue. Four streets actually converge here: Melrose, Park, Brooks, and 165th Street. To stay on Melrose, which becomes Park once you pass through the intersection, follow the bike lane and veer slightly right to cross 165th onto Park. Ride on Park along the Metro North Railroad Tracks through the graffiti-tagged vacant lots of Morrisania—where hip-hop pioneer Grandmaster Flash grew up—and enter East Tremont. Not so long ago, these lots propped up the ruins of abandoned buildings with smoke-singed walls and mocking caricatures of potted plants and curtains placed in blown-out windows, the carcasses of discarded automobiles rusting in the parking lots below, up on blocks and stripped to the

bones minutes after being stolen. The buildings have since been razed by the City, the cars removed, but for resident survivors, the image and smell still lingers.

For the neighborhood of East Tremont, an area already staggered by the Cross Bronx Expressway's destruction of much of its real estate and industry, the arson fires simply delivered the knockout punch. All that was left was for the landlords to come in and sweep away the tenants holding out with exorbitant rent increases. Frank's Sports Shop, which has stood on the corner of East Tremont Avenue and Park for eighty-nine years now, is one of the few survivors. Opened in 1922 by Frank Stein as an Army Navy Surplus store, the family-owned and operated business has since expanded to cater to the needs of just about every kind of sports junkie, both amateur and professional. "All the small stores collapsed in the '80s," remembers Eric, who has worked at Frank's Sports Shop for four decades. The store is large and cramped, packed with everything from hunting jackets to baseball jerseys, pool table felt, hiking boots, turf shoes, fishing vests, racks of old school sweatpants; and the storefront window is filled with stuffed raccoons and every color of Chuck Taylor All-Stars Converse ever made. Squeeze-through walkways weave around the piles of merchandise like intricate mazes, and that's just on the first floor. Over the years, has watched his neighborhood decline. After residents were forced out by the fires, "the rents started going up." Frank's, he says, held on because of its size and diversified inventory. The sign outside advertises work clothes, fishing tackle, and guns—which are all the way in the back across from the football jerseys—as well as uniforms for "every sport," except cycling. He looks around the store, which is light on customers, and shrugs his shoulders. "I mean, right now it's empty," he says. "Soon as the weather changes, when it gets colder, they'll be in."

Continue on Park along the train tracks to the traffic light at East 189th Street. Across 189th, Park becomes 3rd Avenue. Cross through the light and follow 3rd one block until it dead-ends at Fordham University's Rose Hill Campus and East Fordham Road. It's a bit out of the

way, but in case you need it, Crosstown Bicycle is located at 33 East 170th Street between Walton and Jerome Avenues.

Founded in 1841 as St. John's College, Fordham University was the first Catholic higher education institution in the Northeast. The Jesuit-minded school offers degrees in over forty programs of study on three separate campuses throughout the state: Rose Hill in the Bronx, Lincoln Center in Manhattan, and West Harrison in Westchester County. In colonial times, the site of the Rose Hill campus was known as Old Fordham Village, after the manor that was built on what was then called Rose Hill. A few blocks away in Poe Park on the corner of the Grand Concourse and Kingsbridge Road stands another Old Fordham Village house: the 1812 cottage in which American poet and author Edgar Allan Poe spent the final years of his life with his wife, Virginia. Then, the cottage was surrounded by rolling countryside, with *Little House on the Prairie* views that stretched as far as Long Island. Today the nearly two-hundred-year-old house is surrounded by a fence and looks out onto the desecrated concrete jungle of the busy divided thoroughfare called the Grand Concourse.

At the university, turn right onto East Fordham Road. East Fordham is another busy thoroughfare, but rideable, although you'll want to steer clear of it during rush hour. If you're hungry, pick up a slice at University Pizza (574 East Fordham), then head out to East Fordham and drop down through the tunnel, making sure to ride on the

white-striped shoulder, past the zoo and botanical garden and onto the Pelham Parkway.

The largest urban zoo in the United States, the Bronx Zoo opened in 1899, with over 800 animals on display for public viewing. Originally, the land was owned by Fordham University as part of its Rose Hill campus. Attempting to insulate itself from the rapid development urbanizing the Bronx, for the basement price of $1,000, the university sold the 250-plus parcel along with a significant portion of what would become the New York Botanical Garden to the City of New York, with the stipulation that it be converted to a zoological park and garden. At present, the zoo exhibits over 4,000 animals, representing more than 650 species, including lions, storks, zebras, gazelles, wild gorillas, monkeys, lemurs, hissing cockroaches, crocodiles, and about 640 or so others.

Across the street, the 250-acre New York Botanical Garden nurtures some of the world's most important plant laboratories, including 50 different gardens, waterfalls, wetlands, and 50 acres of old-growth forest, with over two-hundred-year-old ash trees, river birches, beeches, and tulip and cherry trees. Together, the garden and the zoo comprise Bronx Park, a 718-acre tract of land and mere fraction of some 7,000 acres of parks, natural forest, and wetlands in this oft-maligned borough, approximately one-fifth of its total area and more green space than any other urban environment in the country.

If you are in need of a bathroom, the Visitor's Center in the Botanical Garden (Southern Boulevard entrance) is likely your best bet. Otherwise, continue along East Fordham through the Bronx River Parkway and Pelham Parkway interchange. *Note: Navigating this interchange is tricky.* From the zoo, hop onto the bike path / pedestrian walkway. Follow the path until it dead-ends at the southbound Bronx Parkway on-ramp. Cross the on-ramp (checking first for oncoming vehicles), then pick up the path on the other side. Continue on the path and follow the same procedure three more times, through the SB off-ramp and both NB on- and off-ramps. If you are an experienced rider and feel safe cycling in traffic, after the SB off-ramp, if general conditions are safe enough, ride on the street. Otherwise, merge onto the street once you are safely through the interchange.

When you reach Boston Road, turn left into the far right lane of traffic, then turn right onto the North Bronx Bikeway (Pelham Parkway Greenway) as soon as you cross the westbound lanes of traffic on Pelham Parkway. If you do not feel safe riding through this intersection, dismount your bike and utilize the crosswalks.

Initially only a single road, the Bronx and Pelham Parkway was originally completed in 1911. Lined with American elm trees, as its name implies, the 2.5-mile scenic roadway connects Bronx Park to the wetlands and beaches of Pelham Bay. Redesigned and amended to its present form in the 1930s (three roadways: two west, one east, with two medians of parkland saturated with trees), on Sundays, until World War II, the center roadway hosted weekly professional cycling races.

Ride east along the bikeway through the northeast neighborhood of Pelham Gardens. If in need of a restroom break before arriving at Orchard Beach, Starbucks is located just off the Parkway at 1728 Eastchester Road. If desperate, you can pick up a snack there as well.

Originally part of Westchester, like the similarly christened Pelham Bay Park, Pelham Gardens was named after Thomas Pell, the first European to purchase land here. In all, the original Pell tract totaled some 50,000 acres, with parts of it still existing as Westchester County. Acquired by New York City in the early 1900s, from the turn of the century through the 1970s, the mostly working-class neighborhood's population was Italian American and Jewish. Since then, as with the rest of the City, significant numbers of Puerto Rican, Dominican, Albanian, and Asian immigrants have joined in the mix.

Arguably, the most fascinating house in all of New York City, quite possibly in all the country, is found in this neighborhood. **About one thousand feet after you pass Eastchester Road, cut across the grass median to the north and stop at the corner of Westervelt Avenue and Pelham Parkway North.** The unbelievable "holy mother of all things tacky and wonderful" looming in front of you belongs to Eugene and Nelly Garabedian. More commonly known as the Bronx Christmas House, from a life-size replica of Santa and his reindeer (all nine, including Rudolph and the sleigh), prancing across a specially made second-floor tarmac propped up by fake Doric columns, to the heavenly horses and chariot down on the ground below, the cherubim and seraphim, virgins Mary (yes, there are more than one), St. Theresa, right down to the robed and beatific Savior himself, the otherwise-ordinary two-story red brick frame house is so laden with giant Christmas and religious kitsch that when describing this spectacle, it is difficult to know where to begin. Did we mention the lower level of the house as well as the AstroTurf beneath the chariot covering the front patio is painted pink? And this is only the year-round display. Every year, for three and a half decades now, from Thanksgiving through January 6, with the help of their children, the Garabedians unveil a holiday extravaganza that would leave even Madame Tussaud speechless. Each

year more elaborate than the last. Over a hundred mechanical mannequins—gowned and sequined or otherwise glistening, many of them coiffed and made-up doppelgangers of Hollywood celebrities, including Audrey Hepburn, Rita Hayworth, and Liberace and his piano—move to the bewildering awe of the thousands of visitors who come from all over the world to witness the spectacle. And all—Jesus, the virgin and the saints, as well as Santa and his reindeer—are lit up brighter than Times Square on New Year's Eve, running up an electric bill impossible to imagine

As the Garabedians are owners of a fabric trimming business, all of the gowns and costumes are created by Nelly. In fact, according to Eugene, the entire undertaking was his wife's idea. White haired, hunched, and wrinkled with age, his eyes light up when he talks about the real-life celebrities who have come to see their creation: Mariah Carey, Brad Pitt and Angelina Jolie, Madonna and Lourdes, Joe Pesci, "Bobby" De Niro, and Tommy Mottola. "You know who Tommy Mattola is?" he says.

In the off-season, the mannequins are stored off-site in a warehouse somewhere. The garish display is a perennial gift of thanks for a miracle the family witnessed on Christmas Eve back in 1973. Although the Garabedians decline to reveal the nature of the blessing, clearly it was life altering. So much so it inspired the fabric trimmers to turn their home into an unprecedented homage to Jesus, and Santa Claus, and Hollywood.

Continue on the bikeway until it dead-ends at Stillwell. Turn to the right to cross Pelham Parkway and pick up the bike path on the other side of the road. Continue on the path through the Hutchinson River Parkway on- and off-ramp interchange. Keep straight here. Wait for a break in the traffic, and then cross the southbound Hutchinson Park-

way on-ramp in the same manner you crossed the Bronx River Parkway interchange earlier. If, however, you are in need of a bike shop, follow the path to the right and drop down along the Hutchinson River Parkway. As of this writing, there are no bike shops on Pelham Bay or City Island. Westchester Bicycle Pro at 2611 Westchester Avenue is your last bet until you return. Once you are through the Hutchinson Parkway interchange, you will come to another set of on- and off-ramps for the Bruckner Expressway. Just before the first Bruckner off-ramp, the bike path splits in two, with one path veering off to the right, the other continuing straight and to the left. Follow the path on the left. The general rule is to keep the Pelham Parkway on your left.

Cross over Eastchester Bay on the drawbridge and enter Pelham Bay Park. Over three times the size of Manhattan's Central Park, Pelham Bay is the largest park in New York City. Named for Thomas Pell, in addition to the requisite ball fields and playground, picnic areas, tennis courts, and hiking trails, Pelham Bay is home to two wildlife sanctuaries: the Thomas Pell Wildlife Sanctuary and the Hunter Island Marine Zoology and Geology Sanctuary, totaling nearly five hundred acres of wetlands, natural forest, and glacial deposits from the last ice age. In 1966, the City attempted to create one of Gotham's largest refuse landfills here, second in size only to the former Fresh Kills on Staten Island. Local residents fought it and passed a law forever protecting these lands as a refuge for wildlife.

Ironically, surrounded by salt marshes that date back over ten thousand years, the park's only beach is entirely man-made. Conceived and realized by Robert Moses as the Riviera of Long Island Sound, the popular summer seashore was created by filling one-third of Pelham Bay with landfill and dumping on top of it 1.2 million cubic of sand mined from Sandy Hook in New Jersey and Rockaway Beach in Queens. In this case, one can understand Moses's thinking: Staring out at the bay and Hart Island (Gotham's current potter's field with over eight hundred thousand unknown burials), with Long Island and the Sound in the background, herons and egrets flying overhead, nature should have put a beach here.

At the traffic circle, follow the signs to Orchard Beach to continue onto Pelham Bay, or if you're hungry and prefer boats and harbors to beaches, follow the path to the right and head out to City Island. Bathrooms, if needed, are located at the Orchard Beach Pavilion.

Riding into City Island is like being suddenly transported into a quaint little fishing village off the coast of the farthest reaches of northern Maine, only everybody speaks with a Bronx Italian accent. Home to some of the best seafood and lobster restaurants in the City, Sammy's Fishbox at 41 City Island Avenue is reason alone to make the ride; the fishing boats and cozy harbors are a favorite for filmmakers. Spike Lee's *Summer of Sam* was set here, as was Penny Marshall's *Awakenings*, based on the Oliver Sacks novel of the same name, starring Robert De Niro and Robert Williams. *The Royal Tenenbaums*; *Margot at the Wedding*, with Nicole Kidman; and countless others. With multiple antiques shops, cafés, and handcrafted jewelry stores, a day on the island is like finding a treasure chest of ancient wonders in your grandfather's attic. One could get lost here. Hungry for something other than seafood? Filomena's Pizza and Pasta serves everything from slices to manicotti, soups, sausage rolls, traditional Italian chicken dishes, grilled chicken with sautéed broccoli or spinach with garlic for the health conscious;, and every item on the menu is under $20. Your palate's not feeling pizza either? The 1.5-mile island is packed with over thirty restaurants, and every last one of them has restrooms. Ride around awhile; you'll find something.

When you can finally pull yourself away, to return, simply ride north on City Island Avenue back the way you came. Follow the traffic circle around toward Orchard Beach, then pick up the westbound bikeway on the north side of the parking lot to head back to the City.

ON THE WHEEL

NAME: EDWIN GONZALEZ
AGE: 46

OCCUPATION: PET SHOP MANAGER
RIDE: 1952 SCHWINN BLACK PHANTOM. "IT RIDES LIKE A CADILLAC." 1960 SCHWINN TORNADO DELUXE. "SHE FLIES GOOD."

CHAPTER 8

HALLOWEEN—NIGHT RIDE

(Fifteen Miles)

HALLOWEEN

"If you hear the scream of the she faerie at night, you are going to die screaming tomorrow." So goes the ancient Celtic legend of the banshee, a female spirit who appears in the wee hours to foretell the coming of death, particularly in the month of October, the witching month.

For a number of cultures and civilizations throughout the world, Halloween—or some variation or custom similar to it—is the one night a year when the veil between the worlds of the dead and the living all but vanishes, allowing those we have lost to freely cross over and return to us for a time, or, as the Celts believed, for the banshee to come in the dark and snatch your soul. The ancient Celts called it Samhain (Sow-in), as do modern-day witches, meaning "summer's end" in Gaelic, the dying of the warmth and light. To prepare for the dark return of winter, livestock

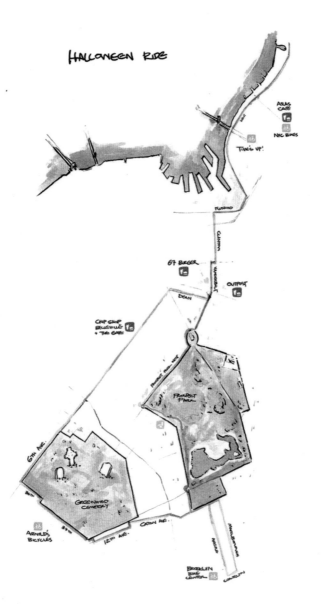

were herded in from pasture to be sheltered or slaughtered, their meat preserved for the bleak lean months that lay ahead. Bonfires were lit to light
the way and welcome in the New Year, which came on November 1 in the
Celtic calendar. Feasts for the dead were held, with place settings and food
laid out to nourish returning souls. As for the night before Hallowmas, or
the feast of All Saints' Day, sometime after the Roman Empire's conquest
of the pagan Celts, the Catholics adopted the occasion as All Hallows Eve,
with a another feast held on the second day of November to honor all
souls, not just those beatified in heaven. Meanwhile, right around the time
the wayward Celtic Church was being reeled back into the boat, some
5,300 miles away (approx. 8500 kilometers), the Aztecs were giving birth
to the modern-day Mexican tradition Día de los Muertos (now celebrated,
like All Souls' Day, on November 2), on which masks are worn and altars
constructed from the photographs, personal items, and favorite foods of
deceased friends and relatives.

In Hong Kong it is called Yue Lan, or the Festival of the Hungry
Ghosts (also celebrated in August), a twenty-four-hour period), during
which adherents sometimes burn money and pictures of fruit, hoping to
appease the spirits who have returned to wander the earth. The Japanese
remember their dead with the Obon Festival, for which special foods are
prepared and red lanterns, with candles inside, were hung about and cast
out to float on the sea. Similar to the practice of Celts, fires are lit to light
the way for returning souls to find their families. In Korea, it is called
Chusok. For witches and Wiccans, young and old, the night is considered
the greatest of all the Sabbats. Independently of each other, it seems, we all
arrived at similar beliefs.

In addition to fires and feasts, early rituals accompanying the Celtic
tradition included the donning of costumes and disguises to prevent rec-
ognition by wandering souls in search of living bodies to inhabit. Although
the first jack-o'-lanterns were turnips rather than pumpkins (pumpkins
didn't make the scene until famine drove a million or so Irish people from
their homeland to the shores of America), one belief is that hollowed-
out root vegetables were lit with a torch or candle and carried as lanterns

by travelers to light their way and ward off evil spirits. Another tells the tale of the spirit of Stingy Jack, a miserly gambler, boozer, and prankster condemned by God and the devil to wander for eternity the dark, cold no-man's-land between heaven and hell, with nothing to light his way but an ember of hellfire carried inside a hollowed-out turnip. According to this legend, jack-o'-lanterns were placed on porches not only to combat evil spirits but also to ward off the trickster Jack, whose antics may well have influenced the holiday custom of trick or treat, as the original treat, since replaced by candy, is said to have been liquor. Meanwhile apple bobbing derived from a divination ceremony, considered most prophetic when practiced on Samhain. If successful in trapping an apple in your mouth, why not play out the complete ritual? Peel the apple into a single strip, wrap the peel around your head three times, then throw it over your shoulder. The letter the discarded peel forms upon hitting the ground represents the initial of your true love's name.

So whether you trick or drink, or put on a ghoulish mask, add another ritual to your Hallows Eve plate and take a ride through the neighborhoods to see the different ways the City honors its dead.

The Ride

Start out in Brooklyn at the beginning of the double wide Kent Avenue protected bike lane at the corner Franklin and Quay streets in Greenpoint, Brooklyn. Before Neziah Bliss—after whom neighboring Blissville was named—constructed a turnpike and installed a reliable ferry service here. Green Point, as its name was spelled back then, was an isolated nub on the western shore of colonial Long Island, settled by a handful of farmers whose names still grace the street signs: Calyer, Norman, and Meserole. Bounded on the west by the East River tidal strait, the north and east by Newtown Creek, and Williamsburg to the south, before then the protrusion on what is now the northernmost tip of Brooklyn was inhabited by a band of Lenape Indians called the Keshaechqueren, who, although ostensibly agreeing to sell the land to agents of the Dutch West India Company, did not vacate without a fight.

The first non-native landowner here was Dirck Holgersen, a Norwegian settler whose name also appears in court records as the more Dutch-sounding Volckertszen. Nicknamed Dirck de Noorman in reference to his Scandinavian heritage, Holgersen's farm and fruit orchards took up a mile of waterfront along the East River tidal strait, stretching eastward to Calyer and Franklin streets (one block from the start point). Not long after Holgersen built the first stone farmhouse here, the Keshaechqueren returned and set fire to a number of his fields, including the barns and homes of relatives who had also taken up residence here. After two of his sons-in-law were killed and another one tortured, de Noorman began selling off parcels of his property in hopes of amassing an army of neighbors to help him fight the Indians. Toward the close of the 17th century, when Holgersen died, his heirs sold the rest of his estate to Pieter Praa, a Dutch farmer who owned the adjacent property and patriarch of the Meserole clan. For the next two hundred years, until Bliss married into the family and connected the remote peninsula to the rest of the world by way of his turnpike and ferry service, the Merseroles and a few cousins, who, including the Calyers, amounted to five families, occupied and farmed the whole of Greenpoint.

Once the turnpike opened, which followed what is now Franklin Street, and the ferry service launched, providing regular access to New York (Manhattan), Greenpoint's development was both swift and complete, especially in the industries known as the "black arts"—the fields of printing, pottery, oil and gas, and glass and ironworks, as opposed to those of a more sinister nature purportedly practiced by witches (although there was a time when some of the above industries, in particular the printing trade, were considered the magic of sorcery). The once-lush waterfront, along which you are riding, that gave the point its name was soon replaced by factories and printing presses, the streets leading away from it lined with hastily constructed row houses to accommodate the mostly German and Polish immigrants streaming into town to work in them. In addition to the black arts, thanks to Bliss, the growing peninsula town also had a sizeable shipyard industry, whose main claim to fame was the construction of the USS *Monitor* and other ironclad battleships that served in the American Civil War.

Although the black arts industries and factories, as well as the shipyards, abandoned Greenpoint in the latter part of the twentieth century for less populated coastal areas where raw materials were more plentiful, it was not without controversy. Indeed, the fifty-odd refineries that once operated alongside Newtown Creek both literally and figuratively left quite a stain. In 1978, during a routine flyover survey, the Coast Guard spotted a rather large oil plume rolling through Newtown Creek. Further investigation revealed that from as early as 1866 (when the oil companies raised the first smokestacks here), through 1950, between 17 million and 30 million gallons of oil had seeped into the creek and saturated fifty-five acres of the surrounding landscape, making it one of the worst oil spills in history and the largest in the United States until the Deepwater Horizon rig exploded off the Gulf of Mexico in the spring of 2010. With several lawsuits pending and blame being tossed around by the various companies at fault, the cleanup from the spill has been slow going at best. Although the environmental protection agency recently stepped in to speed things along, just to be safe, for the next decade or so, make sure to fill your water bottles before you ride through the Point.

Head out in the bike lane along the waterfront through Williamsburg as Franklin Street turns into Kent Avenue. Difficult as it is to believe, the Northside of Williamsburg was not always the hive of the trendy and hipsters as it is today. Originally called Bushwick Shore, although a number of enterprises attempted to do so beforehand, Williamsburgh would not latch on to its own identity until 1827, when it was incorporated as a village in the Town of Bushwick. The first speculative venture in the area south of Greenpoint was undertaken by Richard Woodhull, who purchased thirteen acres of land here and named it after the man who surveyed it—Colonel Jonathan Williams, chief of the United States Army Corps of Engineers and grandnephew of founding father and bifocal and lightning rod inventor Benjamin Franklin. Woodhull attempted to entice potential residents by starting a ferry service to Lower

Manhattan, or New York at the time. The ferry service failed, bested by a competing service owned by another speculator; and less than ten years after he purchased the property, Woodhull went bankrupt. Other would-be developers followed, including Woodhull's son-in-law, and also faced financial ruin over the venture, forcing the sheriff to sell the tract at auction. Not until the Wallabout and Newtown Turnpike opened, linking the fledgling village to Brooklyn, would Williamsburgh begin to show signs of life. Like popcorn kernels in a vat of preheated oil, once the turnpike and a new steam ferry service, established by David Dunham, started to pop, in minutes it seemed the town was overflowing with industry and immigrants. Soon after the ferry service, a distillery was born; and by the time the reluctant village was crowned a City in 1852. In addition to the same black arts that populated Greenpoint, everything from beer gardens to pharmaceutical companies and sugar factories lined its shore. Like the village before it, geographically, Kings County's newest city wore three faces: the Northside, from Metropolitan Avenue to North 15th Street (encompassing the first thirteen acres purchased by Woodhull); the Southside, between Metropolitan, Kent, Union, and Flushing avenues; and a Third District, as it was called in 1835, subsequently and alternatively known as East Williamsburg, Bushwick, and more recently as East Williamsburg again, between Union and Bushwick avenues, Flushing, and the BQE, now extended even farther east to Newtown Creek. The young municipality's newfound independence was short-lived, however, for just three years later, the *h* was dropped, and the former City of Williamsburg was absorbed into the growing metropolis of Brooklyn.

While the Northside attracted primarily German and Italian immigrants, following completion of the Williamsburg Bridge in 1903, an exodus of Manhattan's Lower East Side Jews began settling on the Southside, which preceded an even bigger migration before and after World War II by European Jews fleeing the Holocaust, among whom was Rabbi Joel (Yoel) Teitelbaum, founder of Williamsburg's Satmar Hasidim, one of the largest and fastest-growing Hasidic groups in the world. Also lured to the Southside by the bounty of factory jobs here in the 1960s, Puerto

Ricans, Dominicans, and other Latinos alighted on the neighborhood by the thousands. When the bottom fell out of the City's manufacturing sector in the coming decades' economic crisis, leaving large numbers of Williamsburg's Hispanics unemployed, the Hasidic community steadily grew and prospered, and already strained social and racial tensions between the groups threatened to snap altogether. By the mid-1990s, in the aftermath the financial crisis, the Robert Moses era BQE, and public housing projects—which had taken their tolls on industry and housing—much of the WB had been reduced to an industrial wasteland. Artists and creative types took advantage of this after discovering the cheap rents and abandoned warehouse spaces dying for DIY conversions into live/work lofts.

Today, on the Northside at least, those $500/month two-bedroom apartments and funky two-thousand-square-foot industrial lofts, if they exist at all anymore, have gone the way of the artists that used to live in them, pushed yet again to neighborhoods farther out like Bushwick and Redhook and the hinterlands beyond, replaced by $1,500/month studios, with one bedroom and two bedrooms ranging from $2,500 to upward of $3,500/month. For the most part, except for a radioactive chemical plant here or there, the industrial wasteland, specifically along the waterfront, has been sanitized and rezoned, the warehouses demolished or converted into luxury condominiums with private parks and overpriced views of Manhattan. Aside from further increases in their own numbers on the Southside, the Hispanic and Hasidim institutions appear firmly entrenched, with the area surrounding Bedford and Lee Avenues, Wallabout Street and Rodney affectionately known in bike circles as the Shalom Slalom.

In pop culture, the gritty robber baron district cleans up nicely on film, having been featured in the 1973 biographic police drama *Serpico*, starring Al Pacino as the real-life undercover narcotics officer Frank Serpico, who was shot two years earlier during a drug bust at 778 Driggs Avenue just before he was scheduled to testify before the Knapp Commission about the pandemic corruption in the New York City police department. The neighborhood also appears in the film *A Tree Grows in Brooklyn,* Elia Kazan's 1945 directorial debut based the novel by Betty Smith, as well as episodes of the TV shows *24* and *The Sopranos.*

If in need of a bike shop or bathroom pit stop before leaving the neighborhood, you have a couple of options. For bike fixes, Times Up/Traif Bike Gesheft, Yiddish for "non-kosher bike shop," at 99 South 6th Street, between Bedford and Berry, offers the City's first ever twenty-four-hour bike repair vending machine, complete with patch kits, pumps, tubes, brake pads, etc. Or if the shop is closed and you are low on quarters, or lacking in street mechanic skills, NYC Bikes is a bit farther in at 140 Havemeyer Street between South 1st and South 2nd streets. If you wind up at the Havemeyer shop, Atlas Café just down the street at the corner of Grand Avenue has decent snacks and bathrooms; and, of course Bedford Avenue between Metropolitan and McCarren Park is crawling with food and restroom options.

If you happen to be in town, or looking for something cool to do during Bike Month in May, make sure to stop in at the City Reliquary Museum's annual Bike Fetish block party from Noon to Dark, between Metropolitan and Grand Avenues on Havemeyer Street. In fact, whether it's Bike Month or not, if you've never been before and want a truly unique New York experience, a **Bonus Track** trip to the Reliquary itself at 370 Metropolitan is an absolute must!

Follow the Kent Avenue bike lane around the Brooklyn Navy Yard to the BQE and Williamsburg Street SW. Turn right onto Williamsburg Street, then right again onto Flushing. Disembodied spirits abound at the Brooklyn Navy Yard, the perfect setting for a ride-by on Halloween. From the eleven thousand American soldiers and civilians flogged and starved to death in the holds of the British prison ships docked here during the Revolutionary War, to the decayed-beyond-repair officers' quarters on Admiral's Row, roofs caved in, walls collapsed, vines crawling through the floors and windows, to the abandoned marble halls of the Civil War–era naval hospital next door to the mortuary and graveyard, a nineteenth-century assembly line of death, the echoes of lost souls are everywhere here.

Originally a clamming bay for the Lenape Indians, in 1801, the United States Government purchased the yard from a private shipbuilder named John Jackson for the sum of $40,000. Bordered by Kent and Flushing avenues, Williamsburg Street SW, Navy Street, and the East River, the yard encompasses some three hundred acres of filled-in marshland off the Wallabout Bay. The first in a succession of distinctive warships constructed and launched from this site was the USS *Ohio*. After the *Ohio* followed the *Somers*, aboard which the only known mutiny in U.S. history was attempted, when a teenaged midshipman sought to turn the vessel into a pirate ship. Thwarted before they got started, three of the mutineers, including the teenager, were hanged at sea. The event and ensuing court-martial—here in the yard—of the *Somers* captain inspired Herman Meleville to write his famous high seas novella *Billy Budd*. In 1898, after sailing to the Caribbean, the USS *Maine* mysteriously exploded and sank, killing 266 sailors off the coast of Havana in Spanish-controlled Cuba. Though Spain denied culpability, the incident, fueled by pro-Cuban American newspapers which coined the slogan "Remember the Maine! To Hell with Spain!" led to the start of the Spanish-American War. The most famous ship to come out of the yard was the USS *Missouri*, a.k.a. *Mighty Mo*, aboard which the Japanese signed the surrender agreement officially putting an end to World War II. In 1966, after 165 years of continual shipbuilding, employing seventy thousand workers at the height of production during WWII, the naval yard was decommissioned. One year later, the federal government made good on its $40,000 initial investment when it sold the yard to the City of New York for $24 million.

Today, amidst the ghosts and abandoned buildings, the Brooklyn Navy Yard Development Corporation is turning it into a commercial industrial complex, with much of the crumbling Admiral's Row on the corner of Flushing Avenue and Navy Street slated to become a grocery store.

From Flushing, turn left onto Clinton Avenue. Be careful at this intersection; traffic flies by at a pretty good clip. Bicycle Station is located just a few blocks away on the corner of Park Avenue and Adelphi, should find yourself in need of a quick repair.

The only places where wandering souls tend to hover more than decrepit buildings and overgrown graveyards seem to be old mansions, and Brooklyn's neighborhood of Clinton Hill contains more than its share. It is nicknamed the Gold Coast for all the shimmering opulence lining its streets, particularly Washington and Clinton avenues during the late nineteenth and early twentieth centuries. For a time, like most Brooklyn neighborhoods, the Hill's destiny took a wild Jed Clampett–like detour to the lifestyles of the rich and famous before returning to its more humble path.

In 1874, after merging his own Astral Oil Works with John D. Rockefeller's Standard Oil, Charles Pratt, founder of the Pratt Institute (located just around the corner on Willoughby Avenue), decided to use some of his new Standard Oil earnings to construct the manor of all manors at 252 Clinton Avenue in Brooklyn. Although a number of Pratt's wealthy friends and business associates quickly followed the oil baron's lead, the neighborhood truly began to sparkle when Pratt built, as wedding presents, mansions for each of his children across the street from his own. Four of the Pratt houses remain, between Willoughby and DeKalb, as do a number of Gold Coast mansions and equally exquisite row houses, apartment buildings, and churches in the area bounded by Vanderbilt Avenue, Myrtle and Classon avenues, and Fulton Street. All were built during the same period, between 1880 and 1920, and in 1984 were listed on the National Register of Historic places as the Clinton Hill Historic District.

If you fail to catch any of the Pratt family spirits loitering on the old porches or whispering through the trees that line the streets here, you will see plenty of ghouls, ghosts, and goblins a little farther ahead. Depending on the year, you may even spy singing aliens and vampires honing in on the All Hallows Eve act. Since 1994, with the help of a few friends, neighbors, and the Society for Clinton Hill, every October 31, Janna Kennedy Hyten, a.k.a. the Halloween Lady, turns her 313 Clinton Avenue home and lawn into a hell house extravaganza. In recent years, the owners of numbers 315 and 321 have also joined in the fright night, serving up everything from fake tombstones splayed across the lawns, carnage carnivals, and "musi-ghouls" complete with costumes, sets, and dance numbers the envy of Broadway. So time your ride right! The diabolic spectacle gets under way at 5:30 PM, with performances repeated throughout the night until nine.

From the hell house, cross Lafayette Avenue on Clinton and roll right at the next intersection onto Greene Avenue, followed by a left at the first light onto Vanderbilt Avenue. If you are hungry, Fulton Street, about a block south of Greene, offers a number of options from west to east, including 67 Burger at 67 Lafayette in historic Fort Greene (home of Fort Greene Park, the oldest in Brooklyn, and the Prison Ship Martyrs Monument), to the Outpost Café at 1014 Fulton between Grand and Classon avenues. Both also provide public restrooms, but you should buy something first. Otherwise, continue along Vanderbilt across Fulton and Atlantic Avenue through Prospect Heights to the Grand Army Plaza Traffic Circle, turning right onto Plaza Street West. *(Note: Although there is a bike lane on Vanderbilt, traffic is heavy here. Also, remember to ride as close to the outside of the lane as possible to avoid getting doored.)* For bike shop needs, the good folks at Brooklyn Bike

and Board—560 Vanderbilt between Dean and Bergen streets—will be more than happy to help you get back on the road. *(Also, for a history and info on Prospect Heights, please refer to the Fort Tilden / Rockaway Beach ride.)* Circle around Grand Army Plaza on Plaza Street to the light at Union Street. Turn left onto Union, then right at Prospect Park West into the two-way bike lane on the south side of the street, entering Park Slope.

The original home of the Brooklyn Dodgers, when they were still called the Atlantics, these days a bike ride through Park Slope is often like being an extra on the set of *Attack of the Killer Stroller Moms*. But prior to topping *New York Magazine's* list of the most livable neighborhoods in the City, the western slope of Prospect Park—bounded by Fourth and Flatbush avenues, Prospect Park West, and 15th Street—followed the same well-used tracks through wealth, immigration, decline, poverty (sort of), crime, urban renewal, and "revitalization" as the rest of Brownstone Brooklyn. In the 1960s, what had become an abandoned working-class neighborhood caught the eye of the City's lesbian community (often, along with artists and bohemians, the first wave in the tsunami of gentrification). The Stroller Mom caricature didn't arrive until the early 2000s, when, like the Hipsters in Williamsburg they were priced out of Manhattan.

Baby strollers or no, the restored brownstone- and tree-lined streets, complete with antique lampposts lighting the darkened stoops, provide the perfect setting for jack-o'-lanterns, fake cobwebs, and haunting recordings of witches cackling and owls hooting. All that is missing is the Belgian cobblestone and clip-clop of horse hooves. To that end, annually, on October 31, the Park Slope Civic Council throws the biggest Halloween parade and shindig for children in the country. Beginning at 7th Avenue and 14th Street, the route follows historic 7th Avenue north to 3rd Street, turns left on 3rd and finishes at the Old Stone House, a modern reconstruction of a seventeenth-century Dutch farmhouse that survived for nearly two hundred years in this location, including a stint as the Brooklyn Dodgers' clubhouse when they played at Washington Park, watching the neighborhood around it transform from bucolic farmland to urban tenement buildings before literally sinking into the ground, swallowed by landfill. The 1930s replica, a concession by Robert Moses to memorialize the Revolutionary War Battle of Brooklyn, was constructed using stones from the original. The ghoulish Civic Council procession kicks off at 6:30 PM, just past dark, with the Old Stone House After Party rocking out until nine.

Famous stroller moms and dads who've lived in the neighborhood? Steve Buscemi, Maggie Gyllenhaal, John Turturro, and *Law & Order: Criminal Intent* costar Kathryn Erbe.

Hungry? You've come to the right neighborhood. While 5th and 7th avenues have a plethora of offerings for just about any palate, for a quick stop and a good dose of protein and carbs to keep you going, roll into neighborhood favorite the Park Slope Chipshop at 583 5th Avenue on corner of 6th Street.

At Prospect Park West and 15th Street, turn left at the traffic circle, following the bike lane, then left again at the West Drive entrance into the park. Follow West Drive counterclockwise through the park to the Coney Island / Park Circle exit. If needed, public restrooms are located inside the park at Prospect Park West and 11th Street, off the Park Circle exit (Park Circle is the first light before Coney Island Avenue), and on the walking path just after you turn onto Caton Avenue inside the Parade Grounds. Exit the park and follow the bike lane wraparound toward the left to the second traffic light and spin left onto Coney Island Avenue. Follow Coney Island one block past the Parade Grounds and turn left onto Caton Avenue. (Traffic is dense on Coney Island Avenue, so stay visible and remain alert.) Continue on Caton four blocks to swing right onto Argyle Road into Prospect Park South.

"Victorian Flatbush" is the umbrella term for the ten or so neighborhoods lying immediately south of the Prospect Park Parade Ground between Caton Avenue, Anvenue H, and Ocean and Coney Island avenues. Called so for the atypically large single-family homes with lavish front yards, backyard gardens, and koi ponds (in some cases), deep in the heart of Flatbush Brooklyn (synonymous with just about anything but

wealth and Victorians), they come with such equally lofty names as Caton
Park, Fiske Terrace, and Beverley Squares East and West, to name a few.
Depending on your perspective and class standing, none is more obscene
or luxurious than Prospect Park South.

Hoisting the expression "the other side of the tracks" to a whole
new level, Prospect Park South was developed in the early 1900s just
west of the Brooklyn and Brighton Beach railroad tracks alongside
working-class Irish, Italian, and Jewish communities that overtime gave
way to an even poorer mostly West Indian black population. Designated
as a historic district in 1978, the neighborhood bounded by Stratford
and Beverley roads, Church Avenue, and the railroad tracks was the
brainchild of nineteenth- and early-twentieth-century real estate developer Dean Albert Alvord, a Syracuse native who bucked the trend of
row house and brownstone mania eating its way through Brooklyn by
building a neighborhood of stately manors. In 1899, Alvord purchased a
forty-acre tract of land in the middle of Brooklyn Dodger and baseball
country to create what he called a *rus in urbe*, or another kind of "coun-

try in the city." Alvord placed strict require-
ments on his lots, right down to the laying
of the grass and planting of the trees. Potential homeowners submitted building plans
for Alvord's approval and underwent background checks before they were allowed to
buy. All houses must exceed 3,500 square
feet in size and stand a minimum of forty
feet back from the road, with trees planted
every twenty feet along property lines and

in between houses to further the illusion of living on a multiacre estate
in the country in the middle of New York City. The result is an imposing palatial hodgepodge of twenty-plus-room Queen Annes, Colonial
and Greek Revivals, Arts and Crafts, and Italian villas. Sidewalks were
required, separated from the street by curbs and grass medians, the
streets themselves named after well-known thoroughfares in London:
Albemarle, Marlborough, Westminster, Rugby, Argyle, Buckingham,
and Stratford roads, with red brick and concrete gateposts marking the
boundaries to one of the only communities in the City that hires its own

outside security force in addition to the
NYPD.

As would be expected, like Park Slope
and Clinton Hill, Prospect Park South also
hosts a Halloween parade, and a number
of the Houses, as they are known east of
the railroad tracks, dress up like no others
in the City on this historic spine-chilling
night, the owners, going to great lengths to
scare the bejeezus out of the hundreds of
neighboring Flatbush kids who cross the
tracks to trick-or-treat here.

The monster bash kicks off at 4:30 PM
with a gathering at the corner of Westmin-

ster and Albemarle for hot cider and brownies. The parade starts at 5:00 PM, followed by traditional trick-or-treating that generally winds down about 8:00 PM.

When you're ready to move on, take Marlborough, Argyle, or Stratford roads back to Caton Avenue and turn left. Cross Coney Island and Ocean avenues on Caton and then turn left at Green-Wood Cemetery onto Dahill Road, just before Caton merges into Fort Hamilton Parkway. Follow Dahill two blocks and swing a quick right onto 12th Avenue. From 12th Avenue take the second right onto 36th Street back toward the cemetery and turn left onto Fort Hamilton Parkway. Stay on Fort Hamilton for one block only and then roll right onto 37th Street. Follow 37th along the cemetery for the quick 7th Avenue jog around to the right, then left back onto 36th Street. From 36th Street, turn right onto 5th Avenue. Ride north on 5th to 25th streets and the entrance to Green-Wood Cemetery.

For bike shop needs, you have a couple of options: Closer to Prospect Park South, Brooklyn Bike Center is between Slocum Place and Cortelyou Road at 673 Coney Island Avenue, or Arnold's Bicycles is

just off the cemetery past the BMT tracks on the corner of 8th Avenue and 43rd Street.

Ranked by *Time Out New York* as the best place "to get your morbid on," Green-Wood Cemetery is one of the oldest large-scale permanent resting places in the City. Established in 1838, a full decade before New York legislature passed the Rural Cemetery Act, some six hundred thousand residents occupy its 478 acres. Influenced by the country's first park-like cemetery, Mount Auburn in Cambridge, Massachusetts, the burial ground's rolling hills, forested dells, ponds, and flower gardens overlooking Gawanus Creek—now Canal—set the standard for garden cemeteries to come. In addition to the eminent and notorious New Yorkers who elected to be interred here, from Henry Ward Beecher to Boss Tweed, Susan Mckinney Steward, and 1980s art world sensation and bad boy Jean-Michel Basquiat, since its completion, the cemetery has been frequented as much for its calming scenery as it has to visit or lay loved ones to rest.

A testament, perhaps, to the fact that Green-Wood is no ordinary cemetery, since the 1960s, after escaping captivity on a South American cargo flight bound for present-day John F. Kennedy Airport, a community of talking Argentinian monk parakeets, or Quaker parrots, has made its home in the spire atop the Richard Upjohn–designed Gothic Revival 25th Street entrance gate. Listed on the National Register of Historic Places in 1997, followed by Landmark designation in 2006, in addition to guided tours, the cemetery hosts an annual presentation of live theater performed throughout the grounds by Brooklyn's Dance Theatre Etcetera, as well as music concerts and book readings in its historic chapel.

To finish, from the cemetery, follow 5th Avenue back through Park Slope and hang a right on Dean Street. From Dean Street, turn left onto Vanderbilt and return the way you came.

If you decided to forgo the snack options along the way, treat yourself to a well-earned meal at one of the Slope's mixed bag of top-rated restaurants. Aside from the Chipshop, a few of Bike NYC's favorites are the Prix Fixe **(fixed price) special at** Belleville, **the neighborhood's**

Parisian bistro on the corner of 5th Avenue and 5th Street. Also on 5th Avenue, another bistro (this one Latin), Bogata, serves up a fairly potent Mojito in addition to delicious gluten-free empanadas and tacos and other South American delights. If you've had enough to eat and would rather top off the ride with a drink instead, the Gate on the corner of 5th Avenue and 3rd Street across from the Old Stone House, has outdoor seating and is particularly lauded for its beer and whiskey selection. Or, for coffee drinkers and teetotalers, Red Horse Café on the corner of 6th Avenue and 12th Street makes a descent sandwich and pulls a pretty good espresso. The Gate and the Red Horse are also great spots to use the bathroom.

Otherwise, Happy Halloween!

On The	**NAME: KEVIN "SQUID" BOLGER** **AGE: 39**
Wheel	**OCCUPATION: BIKE COURIER** **RIDE: MOTH TRACK BIKE. "FIXED, NO BRAKES;** **THE ONLY WAY!"**

BOMBIN' BROADWAY (ONE-WAY, NONSTOP!) (Thirteen and four-tenths Miles)

Just make sure you hit all the checkpoints!

So you *wanna* be a bike messenger, huh? In Gotham, the Empire! For couriers and fixed-gear riders, the ultimate no-brakes velodrome! Or maybe you just *wanna* ride like one (Poser! Fakenger!), weaving in and out of gridlocked traffic (littered with pushcarts, pedicabs, pedestrians, and horse carriages), grabbing on to the backs of cabs like you're in a Fellini? Buses? SUVs? OK, here's your chance. Take off on your own personal Alleycat race (even more fun with a group of friends), a balls-out sprint the length of the island down the most famous street in the City, not to mention the borough of Manhattan's oldest and longest. From West 218th Street all the way down to Battery Park—a finish line bookended by the George Gustav Heye Center (the New York branch of the Smithsonian Institution's National Museum of the American Indian) and the Brooklyn-Battery Tunnel Vent Building (featured in *Men in Black* as the entrance to MIB headquarters).

No rules. No stopping, except for traffic lights, of course. No other rush can compare. Just remember when crossing through an intersection even when you have the right-of-way, *always pass behind the pedestrians, never in front.*

But for those of you who couldn't care less about NYC bike couriers or the unsanctioned street races (instigated to test one's mettle, confer bragging rights, and ingest a lot of beer), or even Fellini for that matter,

BOMBIN' BROADWAY

Bike Shops:

1. VICTOR'S BIKE SHOP
   BROADWAY BTW. 174 + 175TH

2. MASTER BIKE
   W 77TH BTW BROADWAY + AMSTERDAM

3. CENTRAL PARK BIKES
   W 59TH BTW 8TH + 9TH

4. SBR MULTISPORT
   W 56TH BTW BROADWAY + 7TH

5. CHELSEA BIKES
   W 26TH BTW 6TH + 7TH

6. BICYCLE HABITAT
   LAFAYETTE BTW PRINCE + SPRING

7. CANAL ST. BIKES
   VARICK BTW CANAL + WATTS

FOOD:

8. HUNGARIAN PASTRY SHOP
   AMSTERDAM AVE + 111TH

9. HANBAT
   W 35TH BTW 5TH + 6TH

10. SHAKE SHACK
    MADISON SQUARE PARK

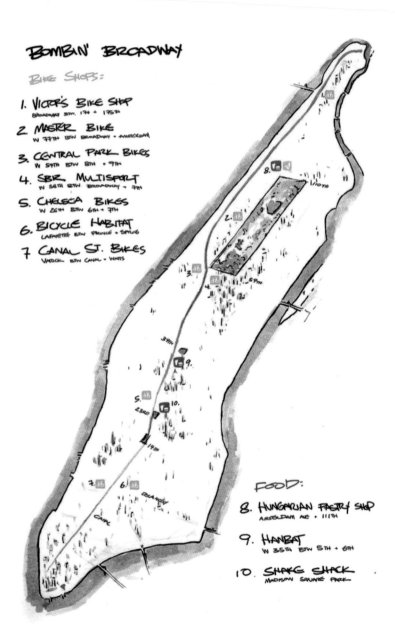

a ride through the storied neighborhoods and history along Manhattan's oldest north/south thoroughfare is still a must.

Breede Weg

A footpath, carved by the Lenape Indians long before Henry Hudson informed the Dutch East India Company of his accidental discovery of the island through which it snaked, the Wickquasgeck Trail, ran from the northern tip of Mannahatta to the southern. Named after the Lenape's Mahican neighbors upriver to the north, Wickquasgeck was the longest of many such trails that ambled over the hills through the forests here. After widening it into a road, the Dutch named the section that ran through New Amsterdam de Heere Straat, or "the Gentleman's Street," then later renamed it Breede Weg, meaning "a broad way."

When the British assumed control of the island, the road found its permanent name in *Broadway*. Although the Broadway that has become synonymous with New York is the only street in Manhattan that, but for a slight jog around Union Square, runs the entire length of the island uninterrupted, only the northern and southern portions of the road follow the route of the old Wickquasgeck. The upper middle and middle segments of the original "broad way," from Washington Heights to the Flatiron District, traversed the east side of Mannahatta rather than the west before cutting back to the center again and forging on to the harbor. Originally, today's Broadway was the Bloomingdale Road in those sections and begins cutting back toward the middle much sooner, just south of Central Park, rejoining the Wickquasgeck at Union Square.

The Ride

Start with a deep-fried sweet, or savory sausage, egg-and-cheese sandwich at Twin Donut Plus (vegetarians, feel free to skip the sausage), on the corner of Broadway and West 218th Street across from the entrance to the Broadway Bridge in the northern Manhattan neighborhood of Inwood. Bordered on the north and east by the Harlem River, the Hudson River to the west and Fort Tryon Park to the south, the area remained largely rural until the 207th Street Subway Station opened, extending the IRT Broadway–Seventh Avenue line to the neighborhood in 1906. Like Harlem before it, Inwood was a neighborhood initially developed on spec, beginning with a bevy of prewar apartment buildings constructed along Broadway, attracting primarily Jewish and Irish residents from lower Manhattan.

Today, like its Washington Heights neighbor to the south, for the most part Inwood is populated by Dominicans. Famous Americans who have called this neighborhood home? Hall of Fame NBA Basketball star Kareem Abdul-Jabbar was born and raised in Dyckman Houses, and much of author / heroin addict Jim Carrol's acclaimed memoir, *The Basketball Diaries*, which was made into a movie staring Leonardo DiCaprio, was written about his life growing up and hustling on some of these same streets.

Home to the only remaining old-growth forest in Manhattan, Inwood is complete with a primordial salt marsh and ancient hillside caves that were supposedly hollowed out by glaciers. In 1626, Dutch governor Peter Minuit executed his famous land grab here, where he traded goods and trinkets worth sixty guilders (about $600 today) in exchange for the island of Mannahatta. In addition to memorializing the "exact" spot where the monumental hoodwink took place, a plaque on Shorakkopoch Rock also remembers a 230-year-old tulip tree that grew here. At the time of its death in 1938, the giant tulip stood 165 feet tall with a girth measuring 20 feet.

At Bennett Avenue, after passing Fort Tryon and the prewar apartment buildings opposite, settle into the saddle for the mile-long climb through Washington Heights. Think about the path that once wound through here. The forests of Appalachian oak and pine, tulip, and hickory shading the way in place of all the brick and mortar. Red-tailed hawks swooping and ravens croaking and perching in the branches overhead. Crows honking instead of cars. The warning screeches of owls replacing police sirens. Squirrels chasing each other's tails around the trunks of maple and chestnut. Hushes of silence, instead of the white noise that is New York, filling the spaces between.

At 173rd Street, the top of the climb, enjoy a well-earned downhill into Hamilton Heights, a.k.a. Sugar Hill and West Harlem. (For Washington Heights lore and attractions, please revisit "return" Option #2 in The Cloisters ride.)

From Alexander Hamilton to Thurgood Marshall, Hamilton Heights (or Sugar Hill as a section of the neighborhood was christened during the Harlem Renaissance), has nurtured and inspired some of the nation's most gifted and creative minds.

The first Europeans to settle here were farmers—a mixture of French, Walloon, Danish, Swedish, German, and Dutch. Incorporated in 1658 by Peter Stuyvesant as part of the village of New Harlem (which, by the way, was called New Harlem because it was the same distance from New Amsterdam as Haarlem is to Amsterdam in Holland), the neighborhood functioned as a battlefield during the Revolutionary War. A number of redoubts were constructed here, and clashes between Continental and British forces were constant. After the war, at the turn of the century, the Bloomingdale Road was extended into the neighborhood and the City's rich—looking to escape the crowded conditions of lower Manhattan— soon began to follow. More than one famous citizen carved out a vast estate in this picturesque countryside. But faced with a rapidly expanding city, country grasses were quickly mowed down by urban concrete.

In addition to Alexander Hamilton's estate, the Grange, which stretched from 140th to 147th streets from Hamilton Place to Hamilton Terrace (the home is preserved today in St. Nicholas Park), James A. Bailey, P. T. Barnum's business partner in the Barnum and Bailey Circus, built a Romanesque Revival mansion, which still stands at the corner of 150th Street and St. Nicholas Place just west of Jackie Robinson Park.

By 1900, Manhattan's population had reached nearly two million people. In 1910, it neared two and a half million, with a population density of 114,000 residents per square mile, more than at any other time in the borough's history. Ever-increasing immigration, a swelling populace, and the rise in development necessary to accommodate it, made the sprawling estates of northern Manhattan's rich obsolete. By the turn of the century, most had been demolished and sold off, replaced with the much smaller row houses and prewar apartment buildings that characterize the neighborhood today.

Famous residents during this period included painter and illustrator Norman Rockwell, who spent a chunk of his childhood at 333 Edgecombe Avenue, and George Gershwin, who along with his brother, Ira, penned a number of today's jazz standards and composed his first hit "Swanny" when he lived at 520 West 144th Street.

Drawn to the light of the creative, cultural, and intellectual New Negro Movement awakening in Harlem, wealthy and successful African Americans began moving into the heights in the 1920s. In this period (commonly known as the Harlem Renaissance), the northeastern blocks were dubbed Sugar Hill, because life was so sweet there. And indeed, it was.

Historically, the decades of the 1920s and '30s are considered Harlem's best. A fruitful and prosperous time—not only for Harlem's black Americans, but for the country's at large—producing unprecedented numbers of the nation's black scholars, political leaders, musicians, writers, and artists of all disciplines, who fed off and inspired each other. Along with Thurgood Marshall, other black luminaries who have called Hamilton Heights and Sugar Hill home include, among others, National Association for the Advancement of Colored People (NAACP) founder, scholar, and *Crisis*

journal editor W. E. B. Dubois; celebrated poet and playwright Langston Hughes; *Invisible Man* novelist Ralph Ellison; boxing great Joe Lewis; and Regina Andrews, the first African American to achieve the position of supervising librarian in a New York Public Library.

Indeed, surrounded by such mind-blowing company, life on Sugar Hill in the 1920s and '30s must have been sweet. So sweet it compelled big band jazz bandleader and swing master Duke Ellington, who lived for ten years at 381 Edgecombe Avenue, to memorialize it in song with collaborator Billy Strayhorn's "Take the 'A' Train," which claimed the now famous subway line as the quickest way to Harlem.

Clearly, Messrs. Strayhorn and Ellington were never acquainted with the bicycle.

Enjoying what many are calling a second renaissance, today Hamilton Heights and Sugar Hill are home to the Harlem School of the Arts and the world-renowned Dance Theater of Harlem. Founded in 1969 by Arthur Mitchell (the first African American to dance with the New York City Ballet), the Dance Theater of Harlem is the country's first African American ballet company.

Bonus Track: If you opted for the leisurely ride down Broadway, rather than your own personal alleycat time trial, and feel like taking a little detour, after passing the Hispanic Society of America, make a left at Trinity Church Cemetery onto West 155th Street, followed by a slight right (as opposed to a hard right) two lights later onto Edgecombe Avenue, overlooking Jackie Robinson Park and Central Harlem. *(Note: 155th is a two-way street with no bike lane. Traffic can be busy here, so remember to stay visible and ride assertively).*

The address of the impressive pre–World War I, E-shaped fourteen-story apartment complex with the ornamental overlays towering above the other buildings on the block is 409 Edgecombe. During the Harlem Renaissance, this was the most prestigious address on the Hill. Through the '30s and the '40s, 409 Edgecombe was home to Thurgood Marshall, painter Aaron Douglas, W. E. B. DuBois, and Eunice Carter (one of the City's first black lawyers and its first black female assistant district attorney). Others who lived on this historic block included story quilt painter Faith Ringgold and pioneering jazz saxophonist Sonny Rollins. **Follow Edgecombe along the bluff above the park and turn right onto West 150th Street to visit the James Bailey mansion on the corner of 150th and St. Nicholas Place.**

To return to the route, turn right onto St. Nicholas Place, then left onto West 151st Street. Follow 151st Street two blocks across Amsterdam and hang a left back onto Broadway.

At 146th Street, the neo-Renaissance building across the street on the northeast corner is the old Hamilton Theater. Constructed between 1912 and 1913, on a design by early-twentieth-century movie house architect Thomas Lamb (Lamb also designed the Regent Theater in Harlem and the Hollywood in Times Square, now both historical landmarks and churches), The Hamilton is one of the last remaining vestiges of the City's vaudeville era. Unlike a number of Manhattan's specialty act theaters (lasting only a few decades before being destroyed or demolished), like most New Yorkers, the Hamilton survived into the twenty-first century due to its ability to change and adapt (a testimony perhaps to the building's designer). From 1913 to present, the structure housed a vaudeville stage, a movie theater, a sports arena, a discotheque, a church, and—at the time of this writing—the El Mundo discount department store (known colloquially as "the hood's Walmart").

From Hamilton Heights drop down alongside the Manhattan Valley Viaduct, listed on the National Register of Historic Places, **into the neighborhood of Manhattanville.** A virgin hollow of dense woods eventually cleared into farmland, tobacco fields, and country estates, the valley you are riding through was known as Bloomingdale (or Bloemendaal as it was called by the Dutch) for most of the seventeenth and eighteenth centuries.

It was here that the Continental Army defeated the British at the Battle of Harlem Heights during the Revolutionary War. Though it is generally agreed that the skirmish held little significance in the overall battle for Manhattan (Washington and his army were soon driven from the island as they had been driven from Brooklyn a month earlier), it is noteworthy because it marked the first time in the New York theater that the Americans had emerged victorious. Just as the miraculous withdrawal from Fulton Landing allowed Washington's army to live to fight another day, psychologically the victory in Harlem Heights lifted morale and proved to the soldiers that they were capable of holding their own against what until then had seemed a daunting and unbeatable foe.

In 1806, where the Bloomingdale Road intersected what was still known as Manhattan Street (the 1811 grid renamed it 125th Street), the thoroughfares of Manhattanville were laid out as the first true "village" of upper Manhattan. Designated yet again in 1984 as Martin Luther King Jr. Boulevard in honor of the slain civil rights leader, Manhattan Street extended all the way to the Hudson River, turning the village of Manhattanville into a thriving harbor town. The village population was made up of an unusual mix of residents from all over the world, including slave traders, slave owners and slaves, anti-slavery activists and abolitionists, free African Americans, Quakers, craftsmen, artists, and the ever-present working poor. As the years went on, the area would follow the trend of most upper Manhattan neighborhoods, shifting from mid-century Irish and German to Jewish after the Civil War, to Cuban, Puerto Rican, and Dominican by the late twentieth century.

Today Manhattanville accommodates a blend of West Side development and expansion by the various colleges and universities located here (Columbia University; City University of New York, CUNY; and the Jewish Theological Seminary). An influx of higher-end restaurants, cafes, and bars cater to the college students who attend them, while several historical churches and synagogues dot the skyline. The historic IRT—Seventh Avenue Line elevated platform stands near the Manhattanville Houses public housing development and the Claremont Theater. One of the oldest movie theaters in the City and currently a self-storage warehouse at the corner of Broadway and West 135th Street, the Claremont was originally constructed to show photoplays, the first produced motion pictures.

At 125th Street and the Seventh Avenue Line elevated platform, relax and get comfy in the saddle again for the climb into Morningside Heights. That's right, another climb. Who started the rumor that Manhattan is flat anyway?

It took a bit of time for the neighborhood atop one of Manhattan's highest natural bluffs to settle on a name. From Vandewater Heights (after the first Dutch colonist to purchase land here), through five other names that included Bloomingdale, Academic Acropolis, and Cathedral Heights, it took years before residents landed on the permanent Morningside Heights nomenclature. Bordered by two parks, Riverside on the west and Morningside Park on the east, and by 125th and 110th streets on the north and south, upper Manhattan's third "Heights" neighborhood remained largely undeveloped through the 17th and 18th centuries. This excludes, of course, the Bloomingdale Insane Asylum, which housed the state's mentally challenged, or "gifted," depending on one's perspective. .

In the late 1880s, after going private and depositing its more impoverished patients in the new state facility on Blackwell's Island, the Bloomingdale Asylum relocated north to White Plains. The institution sold off its city property to Columbia University, the Cathedral of Saint John the Divine, St. Luke's Hospital, and a host of smaller organizations and institutions—all of which were looking to escape the evermore, crowded conditions of lower Manhattan and Midtown.

After Columbia built its present-day campus (as well as the four-acre site of its sister institution, Barnard College), work began, then stopped, then began again on the Cathedral of Saint John the Perpetually Unfinished (as it is nicknamed locally). For the next fifty years or so, Morningside Heights became upper Manhattan's new "it girl" for upper middle-class and affluent white intellectuals.

Post World War II, as more and more Americans—specifically white Americans—fled urban centers in search of their own private Cleaverville in the suburbs (that would be Beaver Cleaver—a.k.a. the Beav as opposed to Eldridge), Manhattan and the rest of Gotham fell into an alarming state of decline. Concerned over the neighborhood's close proximity to Central Harlem, and the unrest and poverty spilling into the "Heights," the trustees of Columbia began purchasing upper west side property around the campus, evicting tenants and leasing the vacant apartments to Columbia students as well as non-students. Eliciting cries of racism from the community, unlawful evictions, and gentrification, the move landed the university on the frontline of a nationwide conflict that had been brewing since Thurgood Marshall forced the country to integrate its public school system. Within ten years, the prestigious Ivy League campus would soon become the site of the worst student riot in the history of the country.

Tensions continued to grow between Columbia and the community of Harlem, widening the divide between the two neighborhoods even further. In the spring of 1968, the conflict came to a head, when Columbia moved forward with plans to build a student gymnasium in a section of Morningside Park. Not only did the controversial plan (which was approved by the City) allow for the building of a private facility on public park land, but its design called for two separate gyms with two separate entrances: one in front for Columbia students and faculty, and one in back for the residents of Harlem. Arguably, the separate entrances were justified from a geographical and architectural standpoint to accommodate the severely uneven terrain on which the facility was to be constructed But given the climate and racial tensions of the day, it was difficult for Harlem residents—as well as the comparatively few black students on Columbia's campus—to see the back door as anything other than a proverbial "servant's entrance." As such, they immediately took to calling the contentious fitness center "Gym Crow."

Compounding matters for Columbia even further, around the same time, in a separate but equally explosive controversy, another group of students discovered that the university was harboring a secret think tank affiliated with the Department of Defense. With the Vietnam War in full swing, igniting a barrage of protests nationwide, at best the new revelation was really bad timing. The two conflicts together proved too much for the college and community to bear, and on April 23, 1968, the outraged students seized control of the campus and staged a massive sit-in and demonstration that crippled the university. By the time it was violently quelled by police one week later, 150 protesters were injured and hospitalized, 700 were arrested, and the acting dean of the university had been held hostage against his will.

Although the actual demonstration lasted only a week, some might argue that the fallout still lingers. While the students succeeded in halting construction of the gymnasium and the university severed its ties with the DOD, today relations between the two communities remain chilly. With demographics shifting in Harlem and Columbia's already–under way city-approved expansion into nearby Manhattanville, band-aids placed over wounds never truly healed have begun to peel off. And once again, cries of discrimination, unlawful evictions, and gentrification can be heard wafting over the Olmsted and Vaux–designed waterfall and turtle pond in Morningside Park.

If you feel like veering off the route again to check out some of the neighborhood sights, Grant's Tomb located on Riverside Drive near West 122nd Street (a.k.a. Seminary Row) contains the remains of Civil War hero and 18th President of the United States Ulysses S. Grant and his wife, Julia Dent Grant. The mausoleum stands directly across from Riverside Church, the tallest church in the country. While you're over there, you can also pay a visit to the Manhattan School of Music a block away on West 123rd Street and Broadway.

To use the restroom or satisfy your snack or coffee jones, stop in at the Hungarian Pastry Shop across from the Cathedral Church of St. John the Divine, at 111th Street and Amsterdam Avenue, and wash down an old-world strudel with coffee that's just as good as at your local diner, only stronger. Bathrooms are available in both the pastry shop and the cathedral.

If you're in town in the spring, every April for thirteen years running now, the church hosts an annual Blessing of the Bicycles. NYC cyclists are invited to bring their bikes inside the cathedral for a short service performed by Reverend "Tom," who anoints our bikes with holy water and offers a few protective words to safeguard our passage through the City.

After the blessing (and a pre-service continental doughnut breakfast), we take a customary lap around the cathedral before spinning back into our lives.

Don't let the holy water fool you. Unlike any other church in the world, the doors of the Cathedral Church of St. John the Divine are open to everybody, secular and religious alike. (Sting even performed in a concert here once.) Regardless of affiliation or belief, the Blessing of the Bicycles is a fun-filled community event in which participants take from it what they wish, as well as a great time to meet and share a free doughnut or two with some of your fellow New York bikers. Plus, layered in at least five different building styles from Byzantine-Romanesque to French, English, and Spanish Gothic to Gothic Revival, the largest cathedral in the world is an architectural wonder that should not be missed.

From the cathedral, or the pastry shop, return to Broadway via 111th Street and turn left to continue down the route into the Upper West Side.

Originally part of the Bloomingdale District (or Bloemendaal in the Dutch), Manhattan's Upper West Side stretches north from West 58th Street to West 110th, and from Central Park West to the Hudson River. Long considered a neighborhood for the City's well-off, the upscale neighborhood is also home to a number of "firsts." The Dakota, for instance (completed in 1884), was upper Manhattan's first apartment building. It was also the site where the first band member of the Beatles died. John Lennon was shot and killed on December 8, 1980, as he was returning home to the Dakota apartment he shared with his wife and son.

As the legend goes, when the City announced the location for the new Central Park, New Yorkers who lived downtown, which was nearly everyone at the time, complained that the designated park land was too far north. With the elevated train lines still over a decade away, working-class New Yorkers had no means to access the park (unless one was rich and could afford to hire a hansom cab, the price of which would have cost close to a week's pay). So for the first ten years or so, the new "Central" Park was deemed a playground for the wealthy. It was so far north, came the cries from downtown, that it might as well be in the Dakotas, meaning the newly acquired Dakota Territories of the United States. Henry Janeway Hardenbergh (designer of the famous Plaza Hotel) and Edward Clark (founder of the Singer sewing machine company and the man who commissioned the building in the first place) supposedly named the first uptown apartment building the Dakota as a play on that joke. Whether or not the legend is fact or myth is not known. For like Dutch Fred the cop (see Hell's Kitchen in Ride 1), no documentation survives from the day to support it. Either way, it makes for a good story. And if you haven't figured it out by now, New York is all about the people and their stories.

At Lincoln Center, cross Columbus Avenue and merge into Columbus Circle at Midtown and the Time Warner Center. This is a tricky and busy set of intersections. Columbus and Broadway crisscross, just as Broadway crisscrosses with 7th Avenue at Times Square, 6th Avenue at Herald Square and 5th Avenue at Madison Square in the Flatiron District. (More on that later.) If you find yourself in front of Fordham University at West 61st Street, you've missed the cross and veered onto Columbus instead. Should this be the case, simply turn left onto 61st, then right onto Broadway to continue along the route.

Initially designed as a turnabout for hansom cabs and other horse-drawn vehicles, the Columbus statue was added to the circle in 1892. Paid for and donated to the City by the Italian American community, the 120-year-old monument was raised to celebrate the four hundredth anniversaryy of the Italian explorer's arrival on the continent. In 1905, a more formal traffic circle was completed around the statue on a design by William P. Eno, realizing Frederick Law Olmsted's original vision of a Grand Circle at the main Eighth Avenue entrance to Central Park.

Stay to the right as you spin around Columbus Circle past 8th Avenue onto the downtown Broadway bike path. Be careful here! Cabs zoom around this intersection like nobody's business, cutting off cyclists and pedestrians as if they get bonus points for it. Remain assertive and deliberate in your actions, and do not be afraid to open your mouth and yell. It is the New York way after all.

If you are in need of a bathroom stop or a bike shop, you have several options in this part of town. Regarding bathrooms in general in Manhattan, there is a Starbucks on every other corner. The bathrooms are private and relatively clean (except for the one on East 14th and Union Square East; might want to steer clear of that one), and you are not required to make a purchase in order to use them. **On Columbus Circle, there are two:** one at the corner of Broadway and West 60th just before you enter the circle, and one on West 58th Street and Eighth Avenue across from Time Warner. For bike shops, SBR MultiSports is located just down the street at 203 West 58th, and Central Bike Shop is a block the other direction at 315 West 57th between 8th and 9th avenues.

The big fat bike path you are riding on is considered a Class 1 lane. We have four tiers of bike lane in the City: Greenways (a la the Hudson River Parkway), which are usually painted green and protected from traffic by a physical barrier other than a row of parked cars; Class 1 lanes, which like Broadway are also separated from traffic, but only by a parking lane and, therefore, still accessible to cars if drivers insist on being jerks about it; Class 2 lanes, the standard set of parallel white lines with the bicycle man stencil painted intermittently between that cars often abuse as parking lots and which pedestrians adopt as extensions of sidewalks; and, finally, Class 3, the so-called shared lanes in which drivers of motor vehicles are expected to be conscious of cyclists and make room for us on the road . . . yeah, right. At the time of this writing, together they amount to nearly seven hundred miles—including parks—of designated bikeways throughout the City, more than in any other city in the country.

The new biking infrastructure—paths like this one are barely three years old—is the result of Mayor Michael Bloomberg's effort, led by transportation commissioner Jannette Sadik-Kahn, in concert with consulting activist and environmental organizations like Transportation Alternatives to reduce traffic congestion in Manhattan and green up the City by replacing some of the six-thousand-plus miles of motor vehicle lanes with pedestrian plazas, walkways, and bike paths to encourage safe, sustainable alternative forms of transportation. Perhaps, if you are old school and bombin' down Broadway like messengers and street racers, or just one of those who prefer the trapped-in-a-Wii-game aspect of riding in the City to the slower-paced Lifetime Movie experience, little of this matters. For the rest of us, flawed as some of the new routes and lanes may be, the effort is truly appreciated.

Ride through Midtown down the new Broadway Boulevard to Times Square. In June of 2009, the section of Broadway that passes through Times Square was closed to vehicular traffic, including that of the two-wheeled variety. From 47th to 42nd streets, you must either walk your bicycle, or use the "shared" lane on Seventh Avenue to ride around it. If you choose the Seventh Avenue bypass, you can pick up the bike path again by turning left at 42nd Street, then right back onto Broadway and the bike lane.

Originally settled as Longacre Square by the Dutch, the area destined to become the "crossroads of the world" and the permanent home of New York's theater district, was primarily farm land. Once the 1811 grid was put in place, the farmers were removed by the 19th century's version of eminent domain. Blacksmiths, horse stables, and prostitutes moved in, and the area soon grew into a bawdy and rowdy entertainment district.

Cigar manufacturer Oscar Hammerstein I, grandfather of the famous lyricist and namesake, in a departure from the established theater district clustered around Union Square, built the castle-like Olympia Theater complex between 44th and 45th streets as the first major theater on the square. When it opened in 1895, in addition to three auditoriums seating more than six thousand people, the Olympia housed a restaurant, promenade, bowling alley, billiards hall, Turkish bath, smoking room, Oriental café, music hall, and a roof garden. Though the Olympia fell into immediate financial trouble and closed its doors just three years later, other show palaces, many of them owned by Hammerstein, soon followed. The Olympa itself eventually reopened under new ownership as the New York Theater, and by the turn of the twentieth century, the new Longacre Square theater district was in full swing.

In 1904, *New York Times* newspaper owner Adolph Ochs, moved the Times' offices into the neighborhood's first skyscraper on the triangle bordered by 43rd Street, Broadway, and 7th Avenue. The ambitious newspaperman then petitioned the City to rename the square after the paper. On December 31 of that same year, Ochs celebrated the birth of the new Times Square by inviting New Yorkers to an all-day street fair before setting off a spectacular fireworks display from the roof of the Times Tower to ring in the new year. A reported two hundred thousand people attended that first New Year's Eve, and the New Times Square never looked back. The first ball was dropped in 1907, and has been dropped every New Year's Eve since, except for the years 1942 and '43, when chimes were rung over a loudspeaker instead due to World War II blackouts.

Believe it or not, the now-famous building wrapped in billboards and giant LED screens, known as One Times Square, is the same building into which Ochs moved his newspaper in 1904. In 1963, new owners Allied Chemical Corporation modernized it, replacing the original granite façade with marble and concrete paneling. Although the tower continued to be leased as retail, restaurant, and office space through much of the latter part of the twentieth century, eventually, the fact that it was operating on what amounted to nineteenth-century wiring and plumbing, and that it is devoid of central air-conditioning made it unattractive to potential tenants. At twenty-five stories high, even renovated, the historic tower would be hard-pressed to compete for tenants against more modern high-rises such as the forty-eight-story Conde Nast tower at 4 Times Square, which houses Vanity Fair magazine, or the fifty-four-floor Viacom building at 1515 Broadway, home to the popular MTV music channel. Realizing they can make much more money leasing the outside instead of the inside, except for the ground level (occupied today by Walgreens Pharmacies), the present owners—Atlanta-based Jamestown One Times Square L.P.—leave the tower empty. It has been empty for years. So how much would it set you back to plaster your face in vinyl on the side of the most famous building in Times square? As of 2008, drum roll please, $350,000 per month. Who needs tenants? And that's just cost of the space. The lighting, the rigging, and custom design often push the expense into the millions.

The Times Square of today is a much more sanitized district than the Times Square of old, washed clean of the grit and grime and crime that once defined not only the square but the entire city.

The decline actually started shortly after World War II. With the advent of television and the increase in talking motion pictures, people were less enamored with live theater and more interested in the little people inside the boxes in their living rooms, or the big people on the larger-than-life screens in the movie theaters. In order to survive, after trying unsuccessfully to covert to movie houses, a number of theaters started showing pornographic films, which ushered in a whole new level of seediness to the district.

By the time the 1970s financial crisis rolled around (leaving the City broke for a couple of decades) and the crack epidemic hit in the 1980s, the area had become your basic red light district, and most New Yorkers steered clear of it. As the City began to find its legs again, and Rudolph Giuliani was elected mayor in the early '90s, a massive and controversial clean-up effort was under way. Loitering and homelessness were made crimes, and overnight it seemed the grit or blight, depending on your perspective, that once characterized Times Square vanished. Where did it go? By most accounts, we loaded it up on buses and drove it to New Jersey.

With the recent recession creating a new crop of homeless, today's Times Square feels a bit more humane, falling somewhere between that squeaky scrubbed-clean illusion of the Giuliani years and the crime and drug infestation of the decades before. Now, if we could just figure out someplace to hide the Naked Cowboy.

Oh, and one more thing: All the billboards and LED screens, etc., around the square are compulsory. In other words, all businesses that lease or own property in the theater district are required by law to display some sort of gaudy, ostentatious, obnoxious signage to contribute to the dazzling spectacle known as the "Great White Way."

Continue along the bike path through the fashion district toward Herald Square. Home to the flagship store of R.H. Macy's, the largest department store in the world as the big red sign on the building boasts (although it is tied in square footage with Harrods of London), the intersection of Broadway, 6th Avenue, and 34th Street was named after the *New York Herald*. During the 19th century, the *Herald* was the City's most popular newspaper.

Shaped like a bowtie rather than a quadrilateral, on the north end of the square at 35th Street, in tribute to James Gordon Bennett Sr., the newspaper's publisher, a monument and small park occupy the real estate where the Herald's offices once stood. The mechanical clock at the top and the bell at the bottom were salvaged from the original building before it

was demolished in 1921. If you are riding through here at night and have the sudden feeling you are being watched, you are. In the dark, the eyes of the owls atop the monument, as well as the two perched at the entrance to the park, light up and glow green.

You might be better off contending with traffic and riding in the street here rather than on the path; more often than not, this part of the bike lane is swarming with pedestrians, both New Yorkers and tourists alike. If, however, you would rather stick to the designated path, Bike NYC recommends you invest in a whistle. In general, bike bells don't really work here. Cars can't hear them, and pedestrians pretty much ignore them. Whistles, on the other hand, tend to scatter them about like roaches.

Across 34th Street, on the south end of the bowtie, lies Greeley Square Park, named after Horace Greeley, publisher of the *Herald's* rival newspaper, the *New York Tribune*. In 1924, in order to better compete with the *Times*, the two papers joined forces and merged to become the New York Herald Tribune, which closed its doors and printed its final newspaper in 1967. The terminus of the Macy's Thanksgiving Day Parade, the square was also the site of the 1947 classic Christmas movie *Miracle on 34th Street*.

Before crossing 34th Street and heading on to the Flatiron District, as you wait for the light, take a look to your left (or to the east), and look up to the sky for a great view and photo op of the Empire State Building.

Completed in 1931, for forty-two years, the Empire State Building was the tallest building in the world. On record as the fastest skyscraper ever built, the 102-story structure was completed in just under fourteen months. A total of 3,400 workers put in 7 million hours of labor, including holidays and Sundays, to maintain the blistering pace of finishing 4.5 floors per week. In the throes of the Depression, New Yorkers watched amazed as John Jacob Raskob's art deco wonder shot into the sky like a rocket; and when the smoke finally cleared, not only had the iconic building gone up faster than any other high-rise in history, it had come in $10 million under budget.

Designed by the architectural firm of Shreve, Lamb & Harmon Associates, initially, the building was only slated to be eighty stories tall. But as New York was in the midst of a skyscraper war—both the Chrysler Building and 40 Wall Street (now the Trump Building) were going up at the same time—the height kept increasing. First to 85 floors, then on the whim of Raskob, a former General Motors exec and the building's financier, to the final 102 to accommodate a spire on top that doubled as a mooring station for dirigibles (airships like the Blimp). Raskob not only wanted his building to be higher than any other building in the world, allegedly holding a pencil up to the building's architects and asking "How high can you make it so it won't fall down," but also for the structure to so far surpass the also-rans in function and form. There would be no question that the Empire State Building was the greatest architectural feat in history. Unfortunately, after endless calculations and consultations with experts, and sixty thousand dollars worth of alterations to existing plans, the docking port never worked. In all their computations, the engineers failed to consider the unpredictable swirling winds caused by the building's severe updraft (due to its great height), and though several attempts were made, no dirigible was able to get close enough to tie up. Finally, in 1937, after the Hindenburg exploded across the river in New Jersey, the plan was scrapped.

Cross 34th Street with the light and follow the bike lane arrows and circular bicycle stencils past Daffy's discount department store (on your right) around the pedestrian plaza to the light at West 33rd Street. Cross Sixth Avenue (also known as Avenue of the Americas) with the light and continue following the bike lane across 33rd Street. If you are hungry, West 32nd Street between Broadway and 5th Avenue represents the heart of Koreatown, or K-town as locals call it, home to some of the best Korean food outside of Seoul. If you have never tried Korean food before, particularly Korean barbecue, you are in for a treat! K-town runs from 32nd to 35th streets between 5th and 6th avenues. It is close to impossible to go wrong here, so pick a restaurant and have at it.

If Korean food fails to float your boat, the Halal carts peppered along Broadway through the Wholesale District offer quick, cheap, and clean fuel. Just make sure the word *Halal*—the Arabic version of *Kosher*—appears somewhere on the outside of the cart.

In need of a quick repair? Chelsea Bicycles is located at 130 West 26th Street.

From K-town, continue down Broadway to Madison Square Park and the Flatiron District. At the time of this writing, with the swanky new Ace Hotel taking up residence on the corner of Broadway and West 29th Street, real estate developers are trying feverishly to rename the no-man's-land of Manhattan between Herald Square and the Flatiron District, NoMad, as in North of Madison Square Park. Who knows? Like SoHo, TriBeCa, NoHo, NoLita and DUMBO before it, by publication the transient acronym may have found a home and become a household name. Or at least be included on the official map of New York. For now, however, colloquially, it is still known as the Wholesale District for all the discount

jewelry, luggage, and hairweave supply storefronts lining this stretch of Broadway.

But back before it was de rigueur to plaster old city neighborhoods with cute little acronyms and consider them "revitalized," this no-man's-land had another name: Tin Pan Alley. From the 1880s through the early 1930s, specifically the blocks on 28th Street between 5th and 6th avenues, the area was saturated with music publishers and song composers. The colorful and initially derogatory name is in reference to the cheap upright pianos the publishers kept in their offices, and the harsh, often out-of-tune sounds the pianos emitted as composers auditioned new songs, hoping to get them published. The noise was so grating and deafening, apparently, it drove *New York Herald* newspaper reporter Monroe Rosenfeld to complain that rather than music, it sounded like a hundred people banging on tin pans.

Follow the bike lane and Broadway as it wraps around in front of the Flatiron Building and crosses 5th Avenue. Arguably, the most filmed and photographed building in New York, the Fuller Building, or Flatiron as it is nicknamed, was designed by Chicago World's Fair (Columbian Exhibition) mastermind, Daniel Burnham. At the time of its completion in 1902, at twenty-two stories high, the Flatiron was the third tallest building in the City behind the American Tract Society Building on Nassau Street (twenty-three stories), and the Park Row Building on Avenue of the Finest (twenty-six stories), and is therefore considered one of the City's first skyscrapers.

This district is also known as Madison Square Park, for the park adjacent, named after James Madison, the fourth President of the United States. A couple of other buildings worth mentioning in the neighborhood include the MetLife clock tower (when the Woolworth building was completed), the tallest building in the world from 1909 to 1913. The entirely glass high-rise across from the park on 23rd Street is the newest skyscraper to lay down roots in the neighborhood. Constructed on top of another building and nicknamed the Beanstalk, One Madison Park was completed in May 2009. If you passed on sampling the barbecue in K-town, or are still hungry, the Shake Shack, located in the park's southeast corner at Madison Avenue and East 23rd Street, serves up some of the best burgers in the City. Be prepared to wait though if you are compelled to try one. Since the burger joint opened in 2004, initiates have been known to stand in line for upward of two hours. Yes, hours. The burgers are that good. These days, after mounting a webcam on the roof directed at the line and opening new locations farther uptown, the wait is not quite as long, but Bike NYC still recommends giving yourself a good one-hour window.

From the park, you guessed it, keep following Broadway to East 17th Street, then turn left to jog around Union Square. For three blocks, Broadway becomes Union Square East here, but turns back into Broadway as soon as you pass 14th Street.

Contrary to common belief, the naming of Union Square had nothing to do with the Union Army's victory over the South in the American Civil War. Nor was it related to the country's first Labor Day celebration, which was held here on September 5 1882, and attended by ten thousand people. The area of Manhattan bordered by East 17th Street on the north and East 14th on the south, between Union Squares East and West, was named so because it was the intersection of the City's two main thoroughfares: Broadway and Eastern Post Road, the old postal route over which mail carriers on horseback ferried letters and information between the colonial cities of New York and Boston. In other words, it was the hub of Gotham; and in many ways it still is.

A number of various subway lines converge here, as do artists and artisans and farmers. Mondays, Wednesdays, Fridays, and Saturdays, it is the site of the City's biggest green market. With all of the food choices in the area, in addition to the farmers' market and the broad plaza on the southern end, it is also a place where New Yorkers often come to have a snack, kill time between appointments and meetings, people watch, and match their skills against the square's famous Speed or Blitz chess players. (Which usually means wondering what just happened as they empty their wallets of hard-earned money). From November 23 through December 24, the National Historic Landmark hosts a month-long holiday fair and market, and every April it becomes the site of a massive pillow fight. Anyone can participate. Bring a non-feathered pillow to the square at the designated time, and at the signal swing away. Oh, and don't forget to remove your glasses, which might make it even more interesting if you need them to see.

If you are wondering what those numbers are on the wall of what used to be the Virgin Megastore, on East 14th at the south end of the square, it is not the spiraling national debt, nor is it the countdown to New Year's Eve, or the number of people who have died from cigarette smoking as many have guessed. It is an art installation and digital clock titled The Metronome. Created in 1999, by Kristen Jones and Andrew Ginzel, the clock represents the passage of time in relation to midnight. From left to right, the numbers on the left side of the clock depict in military time the hours, minutes and seconds past midnight—in other words, the time of day. The numbers on the right, reading from right to left, reflect the hours, minutes, and seconds remaining in the day, or until we return to midnight. While the numbers in the middle mean little other than the blurring reminder that time is passing.

Follow the wrap around the park past East 14th Street and The Metronome, and continue on Broadway through the NoHo Historic District, across Houston Street, into SoHo. If you've been gone from the City awhile, you're probably asking yourself, NoHo? Historic district? NoHo, which stands for North of Houston Street, was designated an official NYC neighborhood and historic district in 1999, expanded in 2008 to encompass the area between Mercer Street to the west, Cooper Square and Lafayette Street to the East, Wanamaker Place to the north, and Houston Street to the south. Houston Street is pronounced *house-ton* by the way, not *hew-ston*, named after William Houstoun, who from 1783 to 1786 represented the State of Georgia in the Continental Congress. In 1788, Houstoun married Mary Bayard, whose father, Nicholas Bayard III , cut a road through his property and named it after the congressman.

SoHo, on the other hand, has the honor of kicking off the acronym generation of NYC neighborhoods. Shortened from a description on a

1968 planning commission map, the moniker was first adopted by a group of area artists attempting to rezone the commercial lofts in which they were illegally living to what are now commonly referred to as "live/work" spaces. Before that, the area of the City between Houston, Canal Street, Lafayette / Centre Street and West Broadway was known as Hell's Hundred Acres. A term coined by 1950s fire chief, Edward Cavanaugh, for all the hundred-year-old wood frame factory buildings and sweatshops there that constantly caught on fire. The area now known as SoHo lay largely abandoned until the artists moved in, with their artists' lofts and gallery spaces that literally and figuratively put the neighborhood on the map.

The neighborhood is also known as the CastIron District, and in 1973 was designated a city landmark and placed on the National Register of Historic Places. The façades of those same firetraps that inspired the earlier Hades epithet are fashioned of cast iron molds, rather than stone, and a number of the buildings, refurbished inside, with sprinkler systems added, etc., still stand. Completed in 1871 from a design by Thomas Jackson, 427 Broadway, on the corner of Howard Street, is a typical example.

Aside from its CastIron architecture, today SoHo is known as the downtown shopping district, specifically Spring Street, Prince Street and West Broadway, which are lined with such high-end boutiques as DKNY, Marc Jacobs, 7 For All Mankind, Apple, and numerous others.

From SoHo, skirt across Canal Street along the edges of TriBeCa and Chinatown and pass through the Civic Center and Financial District on your way to the finish in Battery Park. (If needed, Canal Street Bikes is only a few blocks west at Canal Street and Sullivan, just before Varick.)

From 1820 to 1885, the northern and easternmost blocks of Manhattan's present-day Civic Center were home to what newspapers and religious leaders of the time decried as the most notorious slum in the world. Whether or not the neighborhood known as Five Points was as murderous and slovenly as depicted in journalist Herbert Asbury's 1928 sensational True Crime chronicle *The Gangs of New York: An Informal History of the Underworld,* is up for debate. But the streets marked on 19th century maps as Wards Five and Six were indeed occupied by the poorest of the City's poor in the kinds of conditions that most often accompany such poverty. Multiple families crowded into gloomy two-room tenements void of windows and toilets and heat in most cases. Sickness and disease ran rampant. As did prostitution and other forms of lawlessness, and whether or not that justified razing it as happened in 1885, is also up for debate. In the end, those whose homes were destroyed were not helped by it, and most, many argue, simply took up similar residence on the Lower East Side.

From the demolished neighborhood's rubble rose the imposing new halls of administration and justice that leveled it. A new jail replacing the original "Tombs" (the infamous nickname given to all Manhattan's industrial prison complexes) at Lafayette, Franklin, Centre, and Leonard streets. Currently, Collect Pond Park and the Criminal Courts building reside there. Foley Square, the County and Federal Courthouses and the fifth and current "Tombs" now occupy the southern blocks of the wards. The forty-one-floor Jacob K. Javitz Federal Office Building towers high above Foley Square. During construction of the thirty-story Ted Weiss Federal Building originally planned across from it in 1991, excavation for the foundation of the building was halted when construction crews uncovered the 17th and 18th century remains of over four hundred free and enslaved Africans buried twenty feet below the surface. After some controversy, the site was designated a National Historic Landmark, the remains reinterred and a monument installed to honor them. The Federal building was moved and constructed in its current location at 290 Broadway on the corner of Duane Street. It is believed that between fifteen and twenty thousand men, women and children of African descent are interred here, most forever lost under the halls of justice and administration, parks and skyscrapers surrounding this very small patch of what is believed a 6.6-acre burial ground of some of the City's earliest settlers.

At Broadway and Chambers Street stands the newly restored Tweed Courthouse, named after the fabled William "Boss" Tweed, the Tammany Hall–elected public works commissioner. Who from 1861 to 1872, oversaw its construction until it was discovered that he and other Tammany

Hall politicians, including the mayor, had been embezzling large sums of money from the City through giant kickbacks received from contractors on city projects. In all, it is estimated that Tweed & Co. bilked the City of as much as $200 million. Adjusted for today's dollar, that number translates to approximately $8 billion. For his efforts, William "Boss" Tweed would die in the Ludlow Street Jail. After he was convicted, it would take the City nine more years to complete the building. Presently, the NYC Department of Education occupies old courthouse. The New York City Hall across the park from it is the oldest City Hall in the country that still houses the mayor's office. The French Renaissance and American-Georgian styled structure, designed by John McComb Jr., and Joseph Francois Mangin as part of a design competition, was constructed between 1803 and 1812. Architect Cass Gilbert's 1913, neo-Gothic Woolworth building at the corner of Broadway and Barclay Street announces your entrance into the **Financial District.** Ironically, the neighborhood with all the money has the worst roads in the City. **Remain alert here!** especially during weekdays. The road is strewn with potholes, and seemingly ongoing construction and the commercial vehicle checkpoint between Cedar and Pine Streets makes for extreme congestion, even by Manhattan standards. The son of a poor potato farmer, Frank Winfield Woolworth epitomizes the elusive American rags-to-riches story. As a clerk in a dry-goods store, he noticed that items that didn't sell were placed on a discount table and marked down to five cents, then lighted on the idea of an everyday low-priced five-cent store. After borrowing the capital to make it happen ($300), his first such venture, opened in Utica, New York, in 1879, went out of business within the year. On his next go around Woolworth expanded his original idea to include ten-cent merchandise, and the concept of the five and dime store was officially born. By 1911, F. W. Woolworth Company, Inc. boasted 596 stores throughout the United States and Canada, and in 1913, Woolworth paid $13.5 million in cash for the now-famous building at 233 Broadway.

Although the Woolworth Corporation sold the building and went out of business in 1997, the ornate tower is no less prominent or visible in the Manhattan skyline. At the time of its completion, the fifty-seven-story building eclipsed the MetLife tower in Madison Square Park as the tallest skyscraper in the world, and held the title for seventeen years, until the completion of 40 Wall Street and the Chrysler Building. St. Paul's Chapel, on the corner of Vesey, is not only the oldest surviving church in the City it is Gotham's oldest public building. Completed in 1766, George Washington worshipped in this chapel; his original church pew is still inside. Constructed of bricks mined from Manhattan schist (the bedrock once prevalent throughout the island), the church has remained in continuous use from the time it opened its doors; and despite its close proximity to the Twin Towers, the little Episcopalian chapel survived the events of September 11, 2001, completely unscathed, suffering not even a broken window. A sycamore tree in the northwest corner of the yard is believed to have absorbed most of the debris. The tree's roots have since been memorialized in Bronze by the sculptor, Steven Tobin. In the aftermath of the destruction, the church served as a round the clock counseling and relief station for firefighter, volunteers and other Ground Zero workers.

If you are a Mickey D's fan, you will probably want to drop in for your daily fix at the only McDonald's in the country that has waiters, real silverware and china, a piano bar, and a doorman to greet you as you enter. The food is the same, but the atmosphere is . . . well . . . a little like your ten year old little brother dressed up in one of your father's suits.

Snap a glance to your left as you pass by Wall Street and Trinity Church, where Alexander Hamilton is buried, to catch a glimpse of the New York Stock Exchange and Federal Hall in the distance. This is the second Federal Hall to stand here. The first, where George Washington was inaugurated as the first President of the United States and first United States Congress passed the Northwest Ordinance, was the original City Hall and was demolished in 1812.

Home stretch! Drop down past the Wall Street Bull as you make your way into Battery Park. In a bold act of Guerilla Art, akin to Philippe Petit's high wire tightrope dance between the Twin Towers in 1974, two years after the stock market crash of 1987, sculptor Arturo Di Modica spent $360,000 of his own money to illegally install his eleven-foot-tall,

7,200-pound (3200 kg) bronze Charging Bull, as it is officially titled, beneath a sixty-foot Christmas tree on the doorstep of the New York Stock Exchange. The behemoth bovine, the artist said, was a holiday gift to the people of New York. As thousands of onlookers stopped to admire and praise the massive bull, Di Modica was on hand answering questions and passing out fliers promoting his work. The City and the Exchange, however, were not so amused; and shortly after it was installed, the police removed the attacking statue and locked it in an impound lot. Under a rash of public protest, the City finally caved and the Department of Parks and Recreation installed the sculpture in its current location.

Welcome to Battery Park! The bruised, battered, and punctured bird dropping strewn sculpture greeting you as you enter used to be in the plaza of the World Trade Center between the Twin Towers. All but the bird droppings reflect the damage it sustained on 9/11. The artist is German sculptor Fritz Koenig, and, artwork is titled *The Sphere*. *The Sphere* was reconstructed and moved here during the clean-up effort as a memorial; the burning of the Eternal Flame next to it signifies that we will never forget the events of that horrific day. Over the years, however, the pummeled sculpture has come to symbolize more than just remembrance. Ten years after two 110-story buildings collapsed on it, *The Sphere* stands here an emblem of the City's unwavering perseverance and our uncanny ability to repeatedly rise from the ashes of diversity and misfortune.

Congratulations! You have just bombed Broadway. To make your way back uptown, we recommend circling around the park to the west to Battery Park City and completing the Cloisters Ride.

ACKNOWLEDGMENTS

First and foremost, we'd like to thank our agent, Amy Tipton; Ann Treistman and Kristin Kulsavage and the rest of the Skyhorse gang; our intern, Delia Sarich; Nick James, our illustrator, as well as all the people who rode with us, gave their time and advice, and shared their stories.

A special nod and shout out to our sponsors for keeping us outfitted and rolling: Grime, Lomography, Spokepunchers, Chrome, Panaracer, Urban Velo, EighthInch, Crumpler, Pearl Izumi, Continuum Cycles, Archive, Seagull, GoPro, Sessions Sprockets, and Brooklyn Brewery.

And we would personally like to thank Harriet Blackman, Shelly Blackman, Jr., Shelly Kirk Blackman, Terri and Milton Blackman, Diana Y. Greiner, Natalie Agee, Molly Chanoff, Madigan Shive, Lee Free, Tai Uhlmann, Tom Ahearn, Jane and Dorian LeCroy, RJ Wafer Dwayne Ziegler, Vickie Starr, Sulyn Silbar, Jeff Zell, Jeff Underwood, Nick Lewis, John "Prolly" Watson, Seth Rosco, Black Label, Meghan Brown, Eddie Gonzalez, Classic Riders, Puerto Rico Schwinn Club, Rich Riski, Jeff Fitzwater, Idamay Vanderburgh, John, Glazar, Joe and Julia Ziegler, Kalim Armstrong, Jonathan Beck, Amy Bolger, John Campo. Bill Di Paola (Time's Up), Steve Ferdman, Kent Giltz, Baruch Herzfeld, Seth Holladay (nycbikemaps.com), Eugene Kahn, Dan Katz, Rob Kotch, Pete Lang, Patrick Lee, Samantha Lobis-Green, Maxwell Lobis-Green, Christophe Jammet, Tony Monroe, Peter Moskos (astoriabike.com), Joe Nocella, Michele

Pirone, David Rankin & Mark Taylor (Rankin & Taylor Law Firm), Elizabeth Rapuano, Britt Reichborn-Kjennerud, Mel Rodriguez, John Rogers, Nick Rozak, Caroline Samponaro, (Transportation Alternatives), Harry Schwartzman, Meredith Sladek, Jenessa Stark, and Nona Varnado.